SOAP OPERA TRIVIA

BEEKMAN HOUSE
New York

INTRODUCTION

What is the secret of soaps? Why do they fascinate? What makes so many viewers tune out their personal worlds every day as they tune into *As the World Turns*? Why do people turn on their answering machines when they turn on *Dallas* so the telephone won't disturb them during the program? How many people do you know who you can't talk to during *All My Children*, or who you can rely on to fill you in on every detail of the day's episode when you are away from the TV set? Or, for that matter, how many people do you know who bought a VCR just so they wouldn't miss their favorite soap?

Whatever the attraction each particular soap holds for its audience, there's no doubt that these stories command a fierce loyalty that few other TV programs achieve. Soap fans are singular in their devotion. And if you count yourself a soap fan, here's the perfect way to test how much you *really* know about the soaps—who's getting married, or divorced, or remarried; who has embarked upon a new affair; who's having a baby (and whose baby is it?); who has died (and isn't there something mysterious about the circumstances?); what quirk of fate (or the scriptwriter's imagination) is bringing lovers together or keeping them apart; who has discovered a shattering secret about his or her parentage or past.

It's all the stuff of the soaps: involving, exciting, appealing. Relive some of the moments, remember some of the relationships from your favorite soaps—past and present—with this wonderful collection of quizzes compiled by authors who are themselves avid soap opera fans. And while you exercise your mind on the questions, feast your eyes on the beautiful photographs, and enjoy the delight of exclaiming, "Oh, yes, *I* remember...!"

DYNASTY

GENERAL HOSPITAL

DALLAS

FLAMINGO ROAD

Trivia Entertainment Magazine is published 12 times a year.

Written by: John Kelly Genovese, Mark Guncheon, Ellen Howard, Frank Lovece.

Cover photos: ABC-TV, CBS-TV, Movie Still Archives
Back cover: ABC-TV, CBS-TV, Movie Still Archives

Photo credits: ABC-TV, pp. 2, 4, 18, 19, 24, 27, 34, 35, 42, 54, 55, 64; CBS-TV, pp. 7, 22, 52, 53, 64; Embassy Home Entertainment, pp. 36, 37; Lorimar Productions, Inc., pp. 3, 8, 12, 22, 31, 55; Movie Still Archives, pp. 2, 4, 6, 9, 13, 14, 15, 16, 17, 19, 21, 23, 25, 26, 28, 29, 33, 38, 39, 40, 41, 42, 43, 46, 48, 49, 51, 54, 55, 60, 62; Personality Photos, pp. 2, 3, 4, 5, 7, 10, 11, 20, 28, 30, 33, 42, 46, 54, 56, 61, 63; Phototeque, pp. 1, 2, 17, 19, 20, 32, 47, 48, 50, 51; NBC-TV, p. 3; NBC-TV/Herb Ball, pp. 16, 45; NBC-TV/Al Levine, p. 6; NBC-TV/Gary Null, p. 16; NBC-TV/Ron Tom, pp. 16, 44; USA Network/20th Century-Fox Television, p. 40

CONTENTS

ALL MY CHILDREN 4
ANOTHER WORLD. 6
AS THE WORLD TURNS 7
BERRENGER'S 8
THE BEST OF EVERYTHING 9
CAPITOL 10
DALLAS 12
DARK SHADOWS 14
DAYS OF OUR LIVES 16
THE DOCTORS 17
DYNASTY 18
THE EDGE OF NIGHT 20
FALCON CREST 22
FLAME IN THE WIND/A TIME FOR US. 24
FLAMINGO ROAD 25
FROM THESE ROOTS 26
GENERAL HOSPITAL 27
THE GUIDING LIGHT 28
HOW TO SURVIVE A MARRIAGE 29
KNOTS LANDING 30
LOVE IS A MANY SPLENDORED THING 32
LOVE OF LIFE 33
LOVING 34
MARY HARTMAN, MARY HARTMAN. 36
ONE LIFE TO LIVE 38
PEYTON PLACE 40
RITUALS 41
RYAN'S HOPE 42
SANTA BARBARA 44
SEARCH FOR TOMORROW 46
THE SECRET STORM 47
TEXAS 48
WHERE THE HEART IS 50
A WORLD APART 51
THE YOUNG AND THE RESTLESS 52
'TIL DEATH (OR THE STORYLINE)
DO THEM PART 54

ANSWERS 56

ALL MY CHILDREN

THE GUIDING LIGHT

ANOTHER WORLD

FALCON CREST

ALL MY CHILDREN (1970-)

1 Who first discovered that Silver Kane was an imposter?

2 Who turned out to be little Bonnie McFadden's secret friend "Willie"?

3 Who was Ellen's first husband?

4 What is Kathleen Noone's (Ellen) pet cause, which was later incorporated into the storyline of the show?

5 What was the connection between Zach Grayson and Marian Colby?

6 In all their years of marriage, Donna and Chuck never had a child together. True or False?

7 What is the name of the autobiographical movie about Erica, based on the book she co-wrote with Mike Roy?

8 What was Silver Kane's real name?

9 What was so special about child psychologist Lynn Corson?

10 During her pregnancy Ann Tyler contracted an illness that resulted in her giving birth to a retarded infant. What was it?

11 Who is little Bobby Warner's real mother?
  A. Sybil Thorne
  B. Betsy Kennicott
  C. Nina Warner
  D. Janice Rollins

12 How did John Palmer Cortlandt die?

13 Who played Harry, Benny's bookie?

14 What was Tom Cudahy's profession before he became owner of The Goalpost?

15 Who was The Cobra and what was that person's connection to Brooke?

16 What was the name of the disco, owned by the Hubbards and the Nelsons, which burned down?

17 What is Langley Wallingford's real name?

18 What accidental crime did Dottie Thornton commit when she was little?

19 Who were the late Phil Brent's real parents?

20 Why did Nick Davis divorce Ann?

21 Name Edna's three husbands.

22 Which one of these characters is Andrew Preston Cortlandt's real father?
  A. Palmer Cortlandt
  B. Ross Chandler
  C. Chase Preston
  D. none of the above

23 What identity did Daisy Cortlandt assume when she returned to Pine Valley to see her daughter?

24 Nina had an affair with Steve Jacobi while married to Cliff. True or False?

25 When Billy Clyde Tuggle (Matthew Cowles) returned briefly to the show in the fall of 1984 and kidnapped Adam Chandler, who played his pen pal turned lover?

ANOTHER WORLD (1964-   )

1 Why did creator Irna Phillips call her new soap *Another World*?

2 What writer saved this initially unpopular show from a quick death at NBC?

3 Who played singer/nightclub owner Leo Mars?

4 Who played Leo's twin brother, Dr. Abel Marsh?

5 Match the characters with their occupations:
   A. Alice Frame
   B. Felicia Gallant
   C. Wallingford
   D. Perry Hutchins

   1. cook
   2. mannequin repairperson
   3. romance writer
   4. doctor

6 In what art form is Rachel most proficient?

7 Name the couple married with Rachel and Mac in a double ceremony.

8 Why did Melissa "Missy" Palmer run away to Chicago?

9 Who is Marley's real mother?

10 Former Mayor Brian Bancroft's son was addicted to _____.

11 Why did Mac disown his daughter Iris?

12 Steven Frame was killed in a helicopter explosion in Australia. True or False?

13 Who was the mysterious Mr. Black who headed Black Hawk Enterprises?

14 Name Jamie's scandalous novel about the people of Bay City.

15 Who shot and killed Dr. Royal Dunning?

16 Who shot and killed devious Alma Rudder?

17 *Another World* was expanded to _____ minutes to boost ratings.

18 Mark's revealing story of criminal corruption in Washington, D.C. was revealed in what magazine?

19 Young Julia Shearer wrote two successful romance novels while actually working for another novelist. True or False?

20 Lily is now a TV show host, but what was her previous occupation?

21 Match the owners with their clubs/restaurants:

   A. Perry
   B. Lily
   C. Leo

   1. The Warehouse
   2. Smiley's
   3. Tall Boys

22 What is unusual about Wallingford's appearance on the daytime show?

23 What was unusual about Cecile's and Sandy's roles on *Another World*?

24 Who was Crystal Lake, the mysterious lady who lived above Smiley's?

25 Name the real mother of David and Jennifer Thatcher's son Kevin.

Leading inhabitants of *Another World*: Mackenzie Cory with Rachel (left) and Iris. Inset: Catlin Ewing.

AS THE WORLD TURNS (1956-   )

1 Dr. Annie Stewart Ward gave birth to triplets on the show. True or False?

2 Name the store that Penny Hughes and Neil Wade founded.

3 Why did Dr. Neil Wade give up his medical practice?

4 Who killed millionaire publisher Whit McColl?

5 Who is the father of Paul, Barb's son?

6 Why was Dee Stewart afraid of making love to Brad Hollister?

7 Match the doctor with the actor:
A. Dr. Paul Stewart
B. Dr. David Stewart
C. Dr. Doug Cassen
D. Dr. Dan Stewart

1. Henderson Forsythe
2. John Reilly
3. Nat Polen
4. Marco St. John

8 What caused young Tom Hughes to turn to drugs?

9 What happened a few days after Elizabeth and Dan's wedding to wreck their happiness?

10 Name Betsy's real father.

11 Who played Lydia Marlowe?

12 Though she's a police officer now, for what job did James Stenbeck hire Margo Montgomery?

13 Match the characters with the actresses:
A. Dr. Annie Ward Stewart
B. Dr. Susan Burke Stewart
C. Nurse Pat Holland

D. Nurse Lyla Montgomery

1. Melinda Peterson
2. Marie Masters
3. Mary Lynn Blanks
4. Ann Sward

14 Match these celebrities with their *As the World Turns* characters:
A. Martin Sheen
B. Margaret Hamilton
C. Gloria DeHaven
D. James Earl Jones

1. Dr. Jerry Turner
2. Jack Davis
3. Sara Fuller
4. Miss Peterson

15 Where is the scheming Karen Haines Stenbeck Dixon?

16 Who is Dustin Donovan's real father?

17 Why did John Dixon fake his own death?

18 How did John Dixon fake his death?

19 Craig arranged for Steve to be accused of stealing something belonging to Whit. What was it?

20 What did Steve and his sister-in-law (and former lover) Andrea Andropolous steal?

21 When actress Meg Ryan left her role as Betsy Montgomery, how did the show's producers handle the appearance of the replacement actress, Lindsay Frost?

22 Though Dr. Bob Hughes was reprimanded for arguing with a heart patient and causing the man's fatal coronary, who had actually been on the other end of the fatal argument?

23 Natalie's husband Ralph Porter died of a drug overdose. True or False?

24 *As the World Turns* was the first half-hour soap opera. True or False?

25 Who is Sierra Esteban's real mother?

The world appears to be turning smoothly (for the moment, at least) for these four characters from the long-running soap.

BERRENGER'S (1985)

1 What is Berrenger's?

2 Where was the series set?

3 What was Danny's real name?

4 What was the name of Simon's late wife?

5 The beautiful Laurel Hayes was burdened by the memory of a traumatic childhood experience. What was it?

6 What was Julio Morales' job before he became clothing designer Julian Morelle?

7 Name Julio's wife.

8 Who was Paul's son named after?

9 How did David Berrenger die?

10 Billy Berrenger was a gambler. True or False?

11 Who was Cammie involved with before she started seeing Billy?

12 What tragedy haunted Shane Bradley?
   A. her husband and child were killed in an auto accident caused by her drunken driving
   B. her ex-husband absconded with their child
   C. as a child, Shane accidentally set a fire in which her family died
   D. none of the above

13 How was Todd Hughes related to the Berrengers?

14 What business was Max Feinstein in?

15 Who was Frank Chapman?

16 What was Danny's purpose in arranging the "date" between Laurel and Chapman?

17 Who was Mr. Allen?

18 What position did Shane hold at Berrenger's?

19 Zach Anders was played by a singer/songwriter whose tune for a 1984 summer movie hit topped the charts. Name him.

20 What was Zach's profession?

21 Simon was in love with his daughter-in-law, Gloria. True or False?

22 What was Trans Allied?

23 Why was Danny out to ruin Berrenger's?

24 Why was Ilene fired from Berrenger's?

25 Who replaced Ilene?

The glamorous settings inhabited by these couples from *Berrenger's* weren't enough to keep this short-lived soap on the air.

THE BEST OF EVERYTHING (1970)

1 *The Best of Everything* was based on:
   A. a made-for-TV movie
   B. a feature film
   C. a novel
   D. a short story

2 What famous "bad seed" portrayed Linda Warren?

3 What was the series about?

4 Which famous movie actress, best known for her film role in *Rebecca*, played the formidable Amanda Key?
   A. Agnes Moorehead
   B. Gale Sondergaard
   C. Joan Fontaine
   D. Joan Crawford

5 What well-known screen and stage actress portrayed Violet Jordan?

6 In what town did the serial take place?

12 As a result of the accident, Anne was left blind. True or False?

13 What was Josh Jordan's occupation?

7 Julie Mannix, who portrayed April Morrison, is the mother of *General Hospital*'s Genie Francis. True or False?

14 April, Linda, and Barbara Lamont worked at:
   A. Key Publishing
   B. Fabian Publications
   C. Tempo Publishing
   D. none of the above

8 Fred Shalimar was Amanda Key's brother-in-law. True or False?

9 What happened to Gary Warren?

15 What position did Mike Carter hold in the company?

16 Why did Barbara leave her husband?

19 What was Ken Lamont's occupation?

20 Who was the father of April's baby?

23 What famous college did Joanna Key attend?
   A. Barnard
   B. Smith
   C. Vassar
   D. Hunter

10 Where did Eddie Perrone work?

11 Anne Carter was an aspiring ballerina until a tragic car accident cut short her career. True or False?

17 Who was April's immediate superior?

18 What fictional New England town did April come from?

21 Why was Kim Jordan in jail?

22 Name the magazine of which Kay Farrow was editor.

24 What finally woke Eddie up to the fact that he was in love with Kim?

25 What was the catalyst which broke up April and Dexter's wedding plans?

Three young career women seeking "the best of everything" sparked the story of this soap.

CAPITOL (1982-   )

1 Actress Constance Towers, who plays Clarissa, is the wife of a U.S. ambassador. True or False?

2 Who first played Myrna Clegg, Clarissa's arch-rival?

3 Why does Myrna hate Clarissa?

4 What was Myrna's first major act of revenge?

5 Executive producer John Conboy is best known for his creative work behind the scenes of what other CBS soap?

6 Tyler is a navy veteran. True or False?

7 To ruin Julie's love toward Tyler, Myrna schemed to have her fall for someone else. Who was it?

8 Why was Julie gullible enough to believe her mother's claims about her true feelings toward Tyler?

9 Who was Gordon Hull?

10 In what athletic competition did Matt McCandless hope to enter the Olympics?

11 Wally is prone to bouts of _____.

12 What caused Wally's problem?

13 Why did Sam throw his son Jordy out of the house?

14 Where does Jordy now live?

15 Myrna paid prostitute Shelley Granger $100,000 to leave Washington forever. True or False?

16 Why was Myrna furious when Kelly Harper appeared?

17 Name Kelly and Trey's son.

18 Name the country to which Tyler was sent on a special rescue mission.

19 Name Sloane's TV show:
  A. *Eye on Washington*
  B. *D.C. Discussion*
  C. *A.M. Washington*
  D. *Capitol Focus*

20 Who made Cheetah pregnant?

21 Who did Frankie Bridges date?

22 Dr. Thomas McCandless is paralyzed from the waist down yet still functions as a doctor. True or False?

23 Who killed gambler/mobster Danny Donato?

24 Who witnessed the shooting but refused to come forward to clear the person arrested?

25 Paula Denning remained in her upstairs bedroom for 20 years. True or False?

Top: Sam "Trey" Clegg III and Tyler McCandless. Bottom: Myrna Clegg and Clarissa McCandless. Right: Leading cast members.

DALLAS (1978-   )

1 What is Miss Ellie's maiden name?
   A. Wentworth
   B. Southworth
   C. Ashworth
   D. Eastworth

2 Which of these women did *not* sleep with both J.R. and Cliff?
   A. Sue Ellen Ewing
   B. Afton Cooper
   C. Marilee Stone
   D. Holly Harwood

3 How many actresses have played Jenna Wade, and who are they?

4 Who shot J.R.?

5 Who shot Bobby?

6 J.R. is little Christopher's real father. True or False?

7 Which of these men did Lucy *not* have an affair with?
   A. Roger, the photographer
   B. Mickey Trotter
   C. Eddie Cronin
   D. Ray Krebbs

8 What was Clayton Farlow's terrible secret concerning his son Dusty?

9 What is the name of the Farlow ranch?

10 Jock Ewing was Ray's real father. True or False?

11 Who was Pamela's real father?

12 How are the following people related to the Ewing clan?
   A. Dave Culver
   B. Kristin Shepard
   C. Katherine Wentworth
   D. Mickey Trotter

13 Cliff Barnes is John Ross's real father. True or False?

14 Name Jenna Wade's ex-husband.

15 Match the actors to their pre-*Dallas* series:
   A. Larry Hagman
   B. Susan Howard
   C. Patrick Duffy
   D. Jennilee Harrison

   1. *Three's Company*
   2. *Man From Atlantis*
   3. *I Dream of Jeannie*
   4. *Petrocelli*

16 Which of these former movie queens never appeared on *Dallas*?
   A. Martha Scott
   B. Barbara Bel Geddes
   C. Ava Gardner
   D. Alexis Smith

17 Who pulled the plug on Mickey Trotter?

18 Kristin Shepard is little Christopher's real mother. True or False?

19 How did Mandy Winger meet Cliff?

20 Bobby is Charlie Wade's real father. True or False?

21 Name the chic department store where Pam worked for a while.

22 What is Dusty Farlow's real name?

23 What modeling contest did Lucy win a few years back?

24 Why was Pam going to marry Mark Graison, even though she wasn't in love with him?

25 Before marrying Ray, Donna had an affair with Cliff Barnes. True or False?

Moments from *Dallas*; and (right) an unusually tranquil gathering of the serial's leading characters.

DARK SHADOWS (1966-71)

1 Why was it so vital to Barnabas that Adam be kept alive?

2 Which piece of music associated with a major character became a late '60s hit?

    A. "Angelique's Song"
    B. "Josette's Music Box"
    C. "Quentin's Theme"
    D. "The Ballad of
       Barnabas Collins"

3 Match the characters and the creatures they played:
    A. Quentin Collins
    B. Cassandra Collins
    C. Tom Jennings
    D. Beth Chavez

    1. vampire
    2. werewolf
    3. witch
    4. ghost

4 What were the Leviathans?

5 Ingenue Alexandra Moltke (Isles) recently figured in newspaper reports of a trial. Name the defendant who faced charges of attempted murder.

6 What connection did Dr. Eric Lang have with Barnabas Collins?

7 What was Reverend Trask's obsession?

8 Which one of these actors played only one role during his or her tenure on the show?
    A. Jonathan Frid
    B. Alexandra Moltke
    C. Lara Parker
    D. Jerry Lacy

9 Twentieth century Jeff Clark and 18th century Peter Bradford were one and the same person. True or False?

10 Tad Collins was Cassandra Collins' son. True or False?

11 How did Sam Evans die?

    Three surprised-looking characters from *Dark Shadows*, a somewhat surprising soap opera.

12 Who intervened in the relationship between Maggie Evans and Joe Haskell, and why?

13 What was it that repeatedly caused Angelique's schemes to fail?

14 Who did Willie Loomis work for?

15 Whose spirit possessed young Tad Collins?

16 On what hit series is David Selby (Quentin) now featured?

17 Besides Josette, who was the great love of Barnabas Collins' life?

18 In 1795, Victoria Winters was burned at the stake as a witch. True or False?

19 Who turned Barnabas into the creature he was?

20 Who turned Angelique into the creature she became, and why?

21 Who killed Reverend Trask, and by what method?

22 What was the name of the local hangout for the town's residents?

23 Why did Barnabas and Julia travel back in time to 1840?

24 What did a resident of Collinswood find in a room in the deserted west wing?

25 What was so unusual about the star-crossed lovers Bramwell and Catherine?

DAYS OF OUR LIVES (1965-   )

1 Tony's nightclub was called _____.

2 Who bought the nightclub from the millionaire?

9 What was placed next to the bodies of all the victims of the Salem Slasher?

10 Who was the Salem Slasher?

3 Match the husbands and wives:
  A. Tom Horton
  B. Doug Williams
  C. Roman Brady
  D. Mickey Horton

11 Doug's real name is Brent. True or False?

12 Marlena's twin sister was played on the show by actress Deidre Hall's real-life sister, Andrea Hall-Lovell. True or False?

  1. Marlena
  2. Julie
  3. Maggie
  4. Alice

4 Why did Neil marry the elderly Phyllis Anderson?

13 Psychiatrist Marlena treated Fred Barton for his _____ problem.

14 What was Jessica Blake's streetwalker name?

5 When Liz and Neil bought Doug's Place they changed the nightclub's name. What did they call it?

6 Name the hospital where the Hortons work.

15 Who played Doug's half-brother, Byron Carmichael?

16 What symbol is used to open and close every show?

7 What illness caused Addie's death?

8 Hope had an affair with Roman. True or False?

17 Who announces the opening theme sentence every day?

18 Song lyricist Barry Manilow helps choose the music for the soap. True or False?

19 Who played Michael Horton?
  A. Bobby Eilbacher
  B. Alan Decker
  C. Wesley Eure
  D. all of the above

20 Actress Elaine Princi played two characters, _____ _____ and _____ _____.

21 What caused Marlena and Don to separate?

22 Before she became a doctor, Marie was a nun. True or False?

23 What caused Marlena and Don to separate?

24 How did Roman die?

25 How does Bo get around town?

26 Name Stefano's symbol.

Top: Tom, Alice, Julie. Bottom: Roman, Marlena, Tony.

THE DOCTORS (1963-82)

1 Name the hospital where the doctors worked.

2 What was Dr. Nick Bellini's area of medical concentration?

3 Though Rex Thompson originated the role, how many actors have played Dr. Michael Powers?

4 A sultry film actress, who is now famous, steamed up *The Doctors* as sexy, scheming Nola Dancy. Name her.

5 Academy Award-winning actress Ellen Burstyn once played Dr. Althea Davis. True or False?

6 *The Doctors* used actual registered nurses in many operating room scenes. True or False?

7 What about *The Doctors'* beginnings makes it unique among daytime dramas?

8 *The Doctors* earned a place in TV history by being the first soap to win what award?

9 Match the characters with their professions:
   A. Sam Shafer
   B. Pete Banas
   C. Brock Hayden
   D. Toni Ferra

   1. lab technician
   2. cattle baron
   3. hospital chaplain
   4. hospital custodian

10 When Althea confided in the hospital chaplain about her failing marriage, what happened?

11 Who put Nick through medical school?

12 When Mike tried his newly invented drug, he suffered from psychedelic effects. True or False?

13 Althea's son Buddy died of _____ _____.

14 How did John Morrison die?

15 In Africa, Ann caught a highly contagious disease. What was it?

16 Who cured her?

17 Brooke Shields appeared on *The Doctors*. True or False?

18 How much money did Erich's kidnappers demand?

19 Who kidnapped Stephanie Aldrich?

20 In the opening announcement, to what was the show dedicated?

21 What was causing Althea to go blind?

22 Though Felicia Hunt looked like a young girl, she was actually a 60-year-old woman. True or False?

23 Though Matt was tried for pulling the plug on Joan's respirator, who confessed?

24 Who found the revealing tape on which John confessed that he had allowed Kathy to die?

25 To what city did Penny run to avoid the surgery which offered a 50/50 chance of successfully removing the tumor on her brain?

26 What kind of medicine did Dr. Steve Aldrich practice?

27 Name the former *Route 66* actor who portrayed Jason Aldrich.

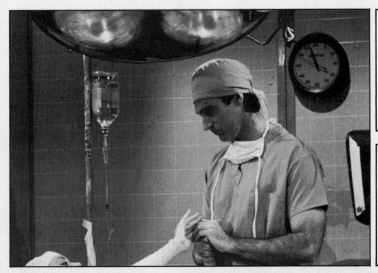

Dr. Althea Davis (Elizabeth Howard) and Dr. Mike Powers (Stephen Burleigh) are two of *The Doctors*.

1 What was the original title of this series?
- A. *Denver*
- B. *Oil*
- C. *The Carringtons*
- D. *Glitter*

2 How did Blake meet Krystle?

3 At the beginning of the series, with whom was Krystle in love?

4 Who is Sammy Jo's real father?
- A. Cecil Colby
- B. Daniel Reece
- C. Mark Jennings
- D. Hank Grant

5 Where was Adam during all those years when Blake and Alexis had no idea of his whereabouts?

6 Who was Blake accused of murdering?

7 What is so unusual about Steven Carrington?

8 Who was Claudia married to before she wed Steven, and what happened to him?

9 Why did Fallon marry Jeff?

10 What subsequently happened to Fallon?

11 Why did Alexis keep Amanda's existence a secret from Blake?

12 Who are little Blake's parents?

13 Who are little Danny's parents?

14 Dominique Devereaux is Blake Carrington's half sister. True or False?

15 How did Cecil Colby die?

16 Jeff married Nicole DiVilbus. True or False?

17 How many children does Blake have?

18 Who was the father of Kirby's baby?

19 Name the hotel run first by Fallon and now by Claudia?

20 Match these actors to their roles:
- A. James Farentino
- B. John Saxon
- C. Helmut Berger
- D. Paul Burke

1. Ahmed Rashid
2. Peter DiVilbus
3. Nick Toscanni
4. Neil McVane

21 Who killed Mark Jennings?
- A. Peter DiVilbus
- B. Alexis Colby
- C. Neil McVane
- D. Blake Carrington

22 What was the tragic secret concerning Kirby Anders' mother?

23 Sammy Jo is Krystle's niece. True or False?

24 What prevented Fallon and Jeff's remarriage from taking place?

25 Which of these women was never involved with Dex?
- A. Alexis Colby
- B. Amanda Carrington
- C. Tracy Kendall
- D. Lady Ashley Mitchell

Dramatic moments from *Dynasty*. Left: A glamorous portrait of leading protagonists Krystle, Blake, and Alexis.

THE EDGE OF NIGHT (1956-75)

1 Serena and Josie Faraday were sisters. True or False?

2 What famous fictional detective was lawyer/crimefighter Mike Karr patterned after?

3 How did Sara Ames die?

4 For whom did mentally unbalanced Emily Michaels mistake amnesiac Draper Scott?

5 Name all Nicole's husbands.

6 Dr. Beth Corell was a 34-year-old virgin. True or False?

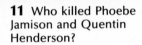

7 Preacher and Jody wed at the series' conclusion. True or False?

8 What prevented Mike's daughter Laurie Ann from making a full recovery in the sanitarium?

9 With whom was Raven having an affair when she first arrived in Monticello?

10 Why was Tiffany Douglas murdered?

11 Who killed Phoebe Jamison and Quentin Henderson?

12 Who was April's mother?

19 How were the murders of Nadine Alexander and Eliot Dorn connected?

20 Beautiful Deborah Saxon chose to be a policewoman. Why was the choice so ironic?

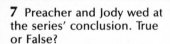

13 How was Elly Jo Jamison killed?

14 Where was Nicole during her year-long absence from Monticello?

21 What happy fact did siblings Paige and Brian Madison discover?

22 What murky fact was in Tracy Dallas' past?

15 At the serial's conclusion Det. Chris Egan was stunned to glimpse Alicia Van Dine. Why?

16 Who kidnapped Raven, and why?

23 Name the man behind the murders of Babs Micelli, Ben Travis, Vic Lamont, and Taffy Simms, and the supposed murder of Nicole (who later turned up alive).

17 What horrible crime did Dr. Eleanor Prentice commit?

18 Who killed Logan Swift?

24 Name the dress shop Nicole originally ran when she first came to town?

25 How did Mike and Nancy's idyllic marriage almost come apart?

Top: Raven and Sky with a well-known guest star. Bottom: Mike and Nancy Karr. Right: Raven again, this time with Eliot.

FALCON CREST (1981-   )

1 How are Richard Channing and Chase Gioberti related?

2 How is Richard related to Emma Channing and Julia Cumson?

3 How is Chase related to Emma and Julia?

4 What is the name of the newspaper formerly owned by Richard, now run by Lance?

5 Why was Lance forced to marry Melissa?
  A. she was pregnant with his child
  B. she was blackmailing him
  C. Angela arranged the marriage so she could get her hands on the Agretti harvest
  D. she threatened to expose a secret concerning the woman he really loved

6 Who was the original owner of the newspaper?

7 What secret did Angela reveal to Maggie?

8 What secret did Angela reveal to Cole which almost prevented him from marrying Melissa?

9 Match these characters with their former spouses:
  A. Linda Caproni
  B. Angela Channing
  C. Victoria Gioberti
  D. Stephanie Hoffman

  1. Richard Channing
  2. Cole Gioberti
  3. Philip Erikson
  4. Nick Hogan

10 Who killed Jacqueline Perrault?

11 Who killed Carlo Agretti?

12 Who killed Sam Giananni and sabotaged the plane carrying most of Falcon Crest's residents?

13 What business are most of Falcon Crest's residents in?

14 Who played Francesca Gioberti?

15 Which of these famous film actresses never appeared on *Falcon Crest*?
  A. Lana Turner
  B. Barbara Bel Geddes
  C. Jane Greer
  D. Jane Wyman

16 Who founded the infamous cartel which threatened to destroy Falcon Crest?

17 Name Terry Ranson's first husband.

18 Name the three characters who perished in the plane crash at the end of the 1984 season.

19 What was the original title of this series?

20 Francesca Gioberti is Angela's half sister. True or False?

21 Name of Chase's late father.

22 How did Richard acquire one third of Falcon Crest?

23 Lorraine is Richard's daughter. True or False?

24 What ex-Playboy bunny appeared on the show as Richard's assistant?
  A. Shannon Tweed
  B. Barbi Benton
  C. Dorothy Stratten
  D. none of the above

25 Match these characters to their unsavory "habits":
  A. Nick Hogan
  B. Gustav Riebmann
  C. Charlotte Pershing
  D. Terry Ranson
  E. Joel McCarthy

  1. drug abuser
  2. call girl
  3. gambler
  4. murderer
  5. married for money

Angela Channing, played by Jane Wyman (seated in the cast portrait) dominates *Falcon Crest*.

FLAME IN THE WIND/A TIME FOR US (1964-66)

1 When the title of *Flame in the Wind* was changed to *A Time For Us*, the central family's name also changed from Skerba to _____.

2 Which character wrote a racy novel about her home town?
A. Leslie Farrell
B. Roxanne Reynolds
C. Louise Austen
D. Kate Austen

3 Was it as *Flame in the Wind* or as *A Time For Us* that this series featured the novelist storyline mentioned in the previous question?

4 In what fictional town was this series set?

5 Jane married rich Steve _____.

6 What role did *The Waltons* star Richard Thomas play?

7 Joanna Miles, Barbara Rodell, and Jane Elliot all played the same role on this show. True or False?

8 Which pairing of role and performer is incorrect?
A. Martha Driscoll— Lenka Peterson
B. Roxanne Reynolds— Rita Lloyd
C. Louise Austen— Josephine Nichols

9 What well-known producer was in charge of this series?

10 What was the familial relationship between Roxanne and Craig Reynolds?

11 Name the medical student played by Terry Logan.

12 What prominent actress played Dave's mother?

13 Leslie Farrell had conceived Roxanne illegitimately. True or False?

14 What role did Lesley Woods play in this series?

15 Diamond-in-the-rough Al Driscoll was played by:
A. Frank Schofield
B. Roy Poole
C. John McMartin
D. Morgan Sterne

16 Irna Phillips created this show. True or False?

17 Name the pianist Roxanne became involved with.

Class conflict and the problems of young love were the themes of this soap.

FLAMINGO ROAD (1981-82)

1 Where was *Flamingo Road* set?
 A. Truro, Florida
 B. Truro, Cornwall
 C. Jamaica
 D. New Orleans

7 Claude Weldon was Skipper's real father. True or False?

8 What was Sam Curtis's occupation?

2 Who was Constance Carlyle's real mother?

3 Who was the father of Annabelle Troy?

4 What did Lane do for a living?

9 Which of these men was married to Constance?
 A. Julio
 B. Field
 C. Sam
 D. Michael

5 What was the name of the town newspaper, and who ran it?

6 Claude Weldon was Constance's real father. True or False?

10 How did Constance become paralyzed?

11 What was Titus's occupation?

12 How was Skipper blinded?

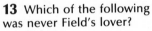

13 Which of the following was never Field's lover?
 A. Lane
 B. Constance
 C. Sandy
 D. all of the above

15 After Annabelle's death, Skipper fell in love with another woman. Who was she?

20 Which of these men was never Lute-Mae's lover?
 A. Michael
 B. Claude
 C. Tony
 D. Sam

14 What was the mysterious connection between Michael Tyrone and Sandy Swanson?

16 What was Michael Tyrone's real name?

17 How did Sandy die?
 A. she was murdered by Michael

21 What was the significance of having a home on Flamingo Road?

22 What was Field's occupation?

 B. she was murdered by Field
 C. she was murdered by Titus
 D. she died from injuries sustained in a car crash

23 Sam was married twice. True or False?

24 For what magazine did Sandy Swanson work?

18 Who committed the crime for which Tom Edwards was convicted and executed?

19 Sam and Lane never married. True or False?

25 There was also a movie named *Flamingo Road*. Name the famous actress who starred in it.

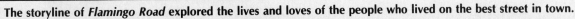

The storyline of *Flamingo Road* explored the lives and loves of the people who lived on the best street in town. 25

FROM THESE ROOTS (1958-61)

1 Name the newspaper that Ben Fraser published.

2 What role did Audra Lindley, star of *The Ropers* and *Three's Company*, play on *From These Roots*?

3 Ben's son, Ben, Jr., rejected the family newspaper to become a:
   A. lounge pianist
   B. farmer
   C. garage mechanic
   D. dog trainer

4 What was the familial relationship between Emily Benson and Nate Tomkins?

5 Liz Fraser was in love with a young man who was confined to a wheelchair. True or False?

6 The *From These Roots* storyline once included a "live" TV production of Flaubert's famous novel *Madame Bovary*. True or False?

12 What role did *The Waltons* star Richard Thomas play on *From These Roots*?

13 How many times did Emily Benson marry?

19 Which now-famous soap villain played mobster Jack Lander on this show?
   A. Larry Bryggman
   B. David Canary
   C. James Mitchell
   D. Joseph Mascolo

7 Liz Fraser and Enid Allen were both romantically involved with the same man. Name him.

8 What role did Robert Mandan play?

14 Fred Barnes, Ben Fraser's brother-in-law, made his living as a:
   A. banker
   B. publisher of a rival newspaper
   C. tractor salesman
   D. criminal lawyer

20 Emily and Nate were patients at what mental institution?

21 Who competed with Liz for the love of her husband David?

9 Which pairing of role and performer is *incorrect*?
   A. Liz Fraser—Ann Flood
   B. Jim Benson— Henderson Forsythe
   C. Luisa Corelli— Dolores Sutton

15 Name the wiley politician played by Leon Janney.

16 *The Facts of Life* star Charlotte Rae played Frank Teton's greedy sister-in-law. True or False?

22 Tom Jennings was a:
   A. theatrical director
   B. doctor
   C. radio station owner
   D. farmer

23 Who did Ben Fraser, Jr. marry?

   D. Dr. Buck Weaver— George Smith

10 Who did Buck Weaver marry?

11 Where was *From These Roots* set?

17 What disease affected actress Lynn Franklin's troubled career?

18 Who played the cocky Tom Jennings?

24 What did the two then do for a living?

25 Veteran actor Frank Campanella played Artie Corelli. True or False?

Top: Liz Fraser, David Allen, Lyddy. Center: Bruce Crawford and Liz Fraser. Bottom: Jim and Emily Benson.

GENERAL HOSPITAL (1963-   )

1 What is Grant Andrews' real name?

2 Felicia Cummings is a princess. True or False?

3 Why did Rick marry Ginny?

11 Why did Holly marry Scorpio?

12 What was the Ice Princess, and why was it so valuable?

4 Match these illegitimate children with their fathers:
A. Jeff Webber
B. Laura Spencer
C. Martha Taylor
D. Jimmy Lee Holt

13 What well-known TV mom plays Felicia's grandmother?

1. Gordon Gray
2. Phil Brewer
3. Steve Hardy
4. Edward Quartermaine

5 Laura once killed somebody. True or False?

14 Bobbie's testimony helped clear Ginny of murder charges. True or False?

6 What was so unusual about tavern owner Sally?

7 Who played Tiffany's agent, Mickey Miller?

8 Heather Webber killed Diana Taylor. True or False?

15 What was the major obstacle which thwarted the romance between Rose and Jake?

16 Alan Quartermaine is illegitimate. True or False?

19 What does Tania Roscov Jones have in common with Grant Andrews?

20 Why did Monica marry Jeff?

9 What was P.J. Taylor's real name?

10 Where was Laura all the time Luke thought she was dead?

17 Who is Jason Quartermaine's mother?

18 What occupation did Bobbie and her aunt Ruby share before arriving in Port Charles?

21 Which of these women was never involved with Scotty Baldwin?
A. Heather Webber
B. Bobbie Spencer
C. Jackie Templeton
D. Susan Moore

24 Match these oddball characters to their professions:
A. Slick Jones
B. Delfina
C. O'Reilly
D. Emma Lutz
E. Stella Fields

22 What is Lee Baldwin's one weakness?

23 What was the name of the spy network for which Grant, Gregory, and Natasha worked?

1. dizzy housewife
2. housekeeper
3. spy
4. dressmaker
5. cab driver

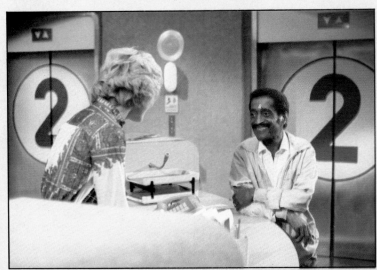

25 Blackie Parrish killed his girlfriend, Lou Swenson. True or False?

Clockwise from top: Luke and Laura; Dr. Rick Webber and Helena Cassadine; Bobbie Spencer; and a top-name guest star.

THE GUIDING LIGHT (1952-   )

1 The character of Michael Bauer was named for the real-life son of actress Charita Bauer, who played the TV Michael's mother. True or False?

9 Why was Susan Piper so intent on making sure that Annabelle and Tony Reardon vacated the cottage they'd recently moved into?

2 Which of these women was never married to Ed Bauer?
   A. Janet Mason
   B. Rita Stapleton
   C. Holly Norris
   D. Leslie Jackson

10 Which of the following was never married to Mike Bauer?
   A. Leslie Jackson
   B. Elizabeth Spaulding
   C. Julie Conrad
   D. Charlotte Waring

3 How did Ed incur the hand injury which, until recently, prevented him from performing surgery?

11 Give Lujack's real name?

12 Amanda Spaulding is Alexandra's sister. True or False?

13 What is Quinton Chamberlain's real name?

4 Which of these Lewis men never married Reva?
   A. H.B.
   B. Josh
   C. Billy
   D. all of the above

14 Match the children with their real fathers:
   A. Amanda Spaulding
   B. Christina Bauer
   C. Victoria Tamerlaine
   D. Billy Fletcher
   E. Stacey Reardon

5 Who are Phillip Spauldings' real parents?

6 Who was Claire Ramsey involved with when she first arrived in Springfield?

   1. Brandon Spaulding
   2. Roger Thorpe
   3. Floyd Parker
   4. Alan Spaulding
   5. Marty Dillman

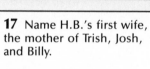

17 Name H.B.'s first wife, the mother of Trish, Josh, and Billy.

18 Trish Lewis has never been married. True or False?

7 Two other fictional towns served as the show's location before Springfield was decided upon. Name them.

15 Which of these actors never appeared on *The Guiding Light*?
   A. Billy Dee Williams
   B. Christopher Walken
   C. James Earl Jones
   D. Christopher Reeve

19 How did Reva meet the Lewis family?

20 What is the relationship between India von Halkein and Alexandra Spaulding?

23 Why did Jim Reardon use an alias when he first came to town?

24 Who stood trial for Stanley Norris's murder, and who was the real killer?

8 Which of the following is Rick Bauer's mother?
   A. Rita Stapleton
   B. Leslie Jackson
   C. Janet Mason
   D. Holly Norris

16 Which of these actresses starred on *The Guiding Light*?
   A. Jobeth Williams
   B. Susan Sarandon
   C. Lee Grant
   D. Jill Clayburgh

21 For what crime was Bradley Raines imprisoned?

22 Who caused Leslie Ann Andrews' death?

25 Beth and Phillip were lovers before Phillip married Mindy. True or False?

Despite the show's title, relationships aren't always clear cut on *The Guiding Light*.

HOW TO SURVIVE A MARRIAGE (1974-75)

1 Dr. Julie Franklin was a:
A. gynecologist
B. surgeon
C. psychiatrist
D. none of the above

17 Which of these character actors played Moe Bachman?
A. Albert Hague
B. Lou Jacobi
C. Albert Stratton
D. Albert Ottenhiemer

18 Which of these actresses, last seen on *General Hospital*, played the Bachmans' daughter?
A. Genie Francis
B. Danielle von Zerneck
C. Robin Mattson
D. Elissa Leeds

19 Dr. Julie Franklin was happily married. True or False?

20 On what daytime soap was Jennifer Harmon (Chris Kirby) last seen?

2 Julie was played by a popular daytime actress who won viewers' hearts as Penny on *As the World Turns* and Amy Tyler on *All My Children*. Who was she?

7 What painful confession did David make to his wife?
A. he was having an affair
B. he was dying
C. his business was going under
D. he had fathered an illegitimate child

11 Name Johnny's wife.

12 Monica Courtland was played by a well-known stage actress who also happens to be the sister of playwright Arthur Miller. Name her.

21 The actor who portrayed David Bachman had a recurring role on *Knots Landing* several years ago. Who did he play?

3 Who was Julie Franklin in love with?
A. Larry Kirby
B. Johnny McGhee
C. Tony DeAngelo
D. Peter Willis

8 What caused Chris and Larry's marriage to break up?

13 This show caused quite a stir when it premiered; what was so unusual about it?

14 Name the two actors who portrayed Peter Willis.

22 Lauren White, who portrayed Maria McGhee, is best known for her role in what other NBC soap opera?

4 Which of these famous *Dallas* stars played Larry Kirby?
A. Ken Kercheval
B. Larry Hagman
C. Steve Kanaly
D. Patrick Duffy

9 What was the name of Fran and David's daughter?
A. Sara
B. Rachel
C. Ellen
D. Jennifer

15 Which of the following actors portrayed Alexander Kronos?
A. Daniel Travanti
B. Brad Davis
C. Tom Selleck
D. William Devane

23 How many actors portrayed Larry Kirby?

24 Michael Hawkins was one of the original cast members of *Ryan's Hope*. Who did he play?

5 What was so unusual about Fran and David Bachman's ethnic background?

6 What business was David Bachman in?

10 What sexy movie and TV star played hot-headed Johnny McGhee?
A. Armand Assante
B. Robert De Niro
C. Al Pacino
D. none of the above

16 What happened to David Bachman?

25 Fran Bachman's second husband was Tony DeAngelo. True or False?

Fran Bachman, played by Fran Brill (center), with her father-in-law and her daughter.

KNOTS LANDING
(1979-   )

1 What is Gary Ewing's greatest weakness?

2 Name the restaurant owned by Richard Avery.

3 How did Cathy Geary come to Knots Landing?

4 How is Abby related to Karen MacKenzie?

5 Which one of these men did *not* sleep with Abby?
A. Jeff Cunningham
B. Richard Avery
C. Greg Sumner
D. Joshua Rush

6 Gary is the father of Valene's twins. True or False?

7 Name the bestseller Val wrote about the Ewing family of Dallas.

8 Who was Chip Roberts?

9 What do Ciji Dunne and Cathy Geary have in common?

10 What famous film actor portrayed Paul Galveston?

11 Who killed Mark St. Clair?

12 How did Abby obtain her variance for the Lotus Point housing development project?

13 What famous film and stage actress portrays Lilimae Clements?

14 How did Mack and Karen meet?

15 How did Sid Fairgate die?

16 Match these children to their parents:
A. Diana Fairgate
B. Joshua Rush
C. Olivia Cunningham
D. Greg Sumner

1. Lilimae Clements
2. Abby Ewing
3. Ruth Galveston
4. Karen MacKenzie

17 What was the Wolfbridge Group?

18 Why was Cathy Geary in prison?

19 Why did Val move to Shula, Tennessee?

20 What was the name of the company Karen's first husband left her?
A. Lotus Point
B. Empire Valley
C. Knots Landing Motors
D. none of the above

21 How did Ray Geary die?

22 What does Ben Gibson do for a living?

23 How many times has Gary been married?

24 Name the four stars of *Knots Landing* who have been with the show since it premiered.

25 Why was Lilimae committed to an institution?

Some of the leading denizens of *Knots Landing*. Left: A wedding day portrait of Abby and Gary.

LOVE IS A MANY SPLENDORED THING (1967-73)

1 Name the actress who originally played Iris Donnelly Garrison and is now seen as a doctor on *General Hospital*.

2 Which came first, the soap or the novel of *Love Is a Many Splendored Thing*?

3 Which came first, the soap or the movie?

4 An affair between novice nun Laura and her sister's boyfriend was written into the story. True or False?

5 This soap presented the first interracial love story seen on a soap. True or False?

6 Why did creator Irna Phillips quit the show?

7 Whose network decision caused Irna to leave?

8 When a drunken Mark raped Iris, who did he think he was really with?

9 What did Dr. Jim Abbott do that caused Mia to end their relationship?

10 When Mia discovered this fact about Jim, she:
  A. married his brother Ed
  B. married his father Kyle
  C. left town
  D. joined a convent

11 What happened to Jim as a result of a medical malpractice suit filed against him?
  A. he was barred from practicing medicine
  B. he lost his girlfriend
  C. he turned to medical research
  D. all of the above

12 What was Mark Elliott's profession?

13 Who originated the role of Laura Donnelly?
  A. June Lockhart
  B. Donna Mills
  C. Veleka Gray
  D. Victoria Principal

14 Tom was accused of murdering Julie's no-good boyfriend Jim Whitman, but who actually killed him?

15 What was Julie's real name, and why did she change it?

16 How did Iris become blind?

17 Did she ever see again?

18 What did Walter Travis use to blackmail Spence in an attempt to force him to lose his senatorial election?

19 Did Spence win or lose the election?

20 Who "owned" Alfred E. Preston, Spence's opponent in the senatorial election?

21 From a ratings standpoint, which of the actors who played Mark Elliott was the most popular?
  A. Sam Wade
  B. David Birney
  C. Michael Hawkins
  D. Vincent Cannon

22 When Laura's scheme to prove Iris an unfit mother failed, how did she fill her own need for a child?

23 Who helped Laura with her custody attempt against Iris?

24 What was Sister Cecilia's original name?

25 In what West Coast town was the soap set?
  A. Los Angeles
  B. Santa Barbara
  C. San Diego
  D. San Francisco

Top: Sisters Iris Garrison and Laura Elliott. Below: Dr. Will Donnelly and Lily Chernak.

LOVE OF LIFE (1951-80)

1 Which of the following actors never appeared on *Love of Life*?
  A. Roy Scheider
  B. Christopher Reeve
  C. Raul Julia
  D. Kevin Kline

2 Which of these famous actresses *did* appear on *Love of Life*?
  A. Lee Grant
  B. Marsha Mason
  C. Ellen Burstyn
  D. Jill Clayburgh

3 Who was Hank Latimer's mother?

4 Why did Ben Harper marry Betsy Crawford?

5 Why was Ben Harper sent to jail?

6 The actor who played Rick Latimer co-starred in the movie *Play it Again, Sam*, playing the ghost of a famous movie star to whom he bears an amazing resemblance. Name that movie star.

7 Who was the father of Kate Phillips's daughter Rebecca?
  A. Rick Latimer
  B. Dan Phillips
  C. Ted Chandler
  D. Jamie Rollins

8 In what town did *Love of Life* originally take place?

9 In what town was the serial set at the time it went off the air?

10 Which of these women was Barbara Sterling's mother?
  A. Vanessa Sterling
  B. Vivian Carlson
  C. Gaye Sterling
  D. Diana Lamont

11 Who was Alan Sterling's real father?
  A. Bruce Sterling
  B. John Dennis
  C. Paul Raven
  D. Guy Latimer

12 Name Vanessa Dale's two husbands.

13 Ben Harper was once raped. True or False?

14 Ben Harper was played by an actor who became an overnight success as a result of one movie role. Name him.

15 Name Meg Dale's two children.

16 What was so unusual about Matt Corby, the man who defended Tess and Bill Prentiss at their murder trial?

17 Who was the real father of Bill Prentiss?
  A. Bruce Sterling
  B. Guy Latimer
  C. Charles Lamont
  D. Charles Prentiss

18 Which of these women married Jamie Rollins?
  A. Diana Lamont
  B. Kate Swanson
  C. Sally Bridgeman
  D. Betsy Crawford

19 How did Charles Lamont become paralysed?

20 David Hart was sent to an institution after committing what serious crime?

21 Which of the following never married Rick Latimer?
  A. Barbara Sterling
  B. Kate Swanson
  C. Cal Aleata
  D. Meg Hart

22 Who was the father of Arlene Lovett's baby April Joy?
  A. Ray Slater
  B. Ian Russell
  C. Rick Latimer
  D. Tom Crawford

23 Felicia Lamont had an affair with Edouard Aleata. True or False?

24 Who was Amy Russell's father?

25 What crime did Betsy's husband, Elliott Lange, commit?

Three person-to-person scenes from *Love of Life*.

LOVING (1983-   )

1 Lloyd Bridges starred in the initial episode of *Loving*. True or False?

2 Name Stacey's best college sport.

9 Where did Merrill first meet Roger?

10 How did Roger die?

11 How did John Madelaine die?

3 Who revealed to Shana the identity of her real father?

4 Who is Shana's real father?

12 Match the characters with their occupations:
A. Noreen
B. Billy
C. Rose
D. Soames

5 What was Garth's position at the university?

6 Who was tried for the death of Garth?

1. butler
2. nurse
3. coach
4. seamstress

13 How did Edy manage to sneak into Doug's locked apartment?

7 Who eventually admitted shooting and killing Garth?

8 Name the Corinth TV station where Merrill Vochek worked.

14 What did Edy always wear to bed when she stayed at Doug's place?

15 Name Edy's closest female friend in Corinth?

16 What drinking spot other than the Hideaway is a favorite of the Donovan brothers?

17 What subjects did Doug teach at the university?

18 Where did Mike finally go to make peace and to try to end the nightmares resulting from his troubles in Vietnam?

19 Who is Jack's real father?

20 Who was Shana's lover years ago in Italy?

21 Why did Tony marry Lorna?

22 Why did Tony divorce Lorna?

23 What did the phrase "burning down the barn" mean to Billy and Rita Mae?

24 Why couldn't Billy and Rita Mae conceive a child?

25 How many Christmas trees do the Donovans decorate in their house during the holidays?

A university town provides the background for the soap opera *Loving*.

1 What made *Mary Hartman, Mary Hartman* different from other soaps?

2 In what town was the series set?

4 What actress, who later starred in *The Big Chill*, played Loretta Haggers?
 A. Glenn Close
 B. Mary Kay Place
 C. Jobeth Williams
 D. Sigourney Weaver

3 Mary's grandfather, Raymond Larkin, was arrested for a crime that earned him a non-too-friendly nickname around town. What did he do, and what was he called?

5 What happened to Dennis Foley just when he was about to make love to Mary for the first time?

6 Which of these women did *not* have an affair with Tom Hartman?
 A. Mona Mackenzie
 B. Mae Olinski
 C. Loretta Haggers
 D. none of the above

7 What well-known Broadway and movie "doll" portrayed Betty McCullough?

8 Ed and Howard McCullough were brothers. True or False?

14 What well-known satirical actor, later to star in the short-lived series *Buffalo Bill*, played Merle?

15 What was Father De Marco's dilemma?

16 Which of these titles was Mary awarded?
A. Typical American Consumer Housewife
B. Mrs. America
C. The Most Understanding Wife in America
D. The Worst Dressed Housewife in Fernwood

17 How did Garth Gimble die?

11 How did Charlie Haggers become impotent?

12 What was the name of the *Mary Hartman* spin-off which starred Martin Mull as a TV talk show host?

18 What happened to George Shumway?

19 Christine Addams died of a heart attack when she learned she wasn't really pregnant. True or False?

9 What prompted TV host David Susskind to invite Mary to appear on his show?

10 What was Merle Jeeter's occupation before he became the town's mayor?

13 Which of these women was *not* bisexual?
A. Annie (Tippytoes)
B. Lila, the Jeeters' maid
C. Wanda Rittenhouse
D. Cathy Shumway

20 Why did Zorina steal Cathy Shumway's baby?

21 What sordid facts were recorded in Wanda's diary?

22 Name the well-known actress, once married to Woody Allen, who portrayed Mary Hartman.

23 By what means did Tom Hartman persuade Reverend Standfast to help him rescue Mary?

24 What horrible crime did Heather Hartman witness?

25 Who was the father of Cathy Shumway's baby?

26 What was Loretta Haggers' big ambition?

27 Where did she first realize that ambition?

28 What happened to Loretta that put her in a wheelchair?

29 What happened to Mary after her nervous breakdown on *The David Susskind Show*?

30 During the final season, Philip Bruns was replaced by Tab Hunter in the role of Mary's father. How was the switch explained on the show?

A study of the assorted characters who peopled the life of Mary Hartman. Inset at right: Mary and husband Tom.

ONE LIFE TO LIVE (1968-   )

1 How many times has Victoria Buchanan been married?

2 Name her husbands.

3 Who is Bo Buchanan's real father?
A. Victor Lord
B. Asa Buchanan
C. Yancy Ralston
D. Chuck Wilson

4 Larry Wolek has been married twice. True or False?

5 When Jenny first arrived in Llanview, what was so special about her occupation?

6 In the early 1970s, what well-known psychologist made several guest appearances on the show to counsel Meredith Wolek?

7 Philip Carey (Asa Buchanan) once starred in a prime-time western series. What was the show?
A. *Lancer*
B. *Laredo*
C. *Bonanza*
D. *The High Chaparral*

8 Who originated the role of Brad Vernon, and what is his latest TV success?

9 What is so special about Delilah Ralston's expected baby?

10 What famous song and dance man had a short stint on the serial as con man Chip Warren?

11 Who is Cassie Callison's real father?
A. Victor Lord
B. David Renaldi
C. Clint Buchanan
D. Herb Callison

12 Who was Nikki Smith and what was so special about her?

13 What do actresses Marilyn Chris (Wanda) and Andrea Evans (Tina) have in common?

14 What was so unusual about the actor who played Lazlo Braedeker?

15 How is Wanda Wolek related to Larry?

16 Who is Drew Buchanan's father?
A. Asa Buchanan
B. Drew Ralston
C. Clint Buchanan
D. Bo Buchanan

17 Name the 1950s movie star and beauty expert who portrayed Lucinda Schnenk.

18 Gerald Anthony played both Marco Dane and Mario Corelli. True or False?

19 An Emmy Award winning actor who also starred in *Coal Miner's Daughter* once played Dr. Mark Toland. Name him.

20 What was so unusual about Carla Gray's engagement to Dr. Jim Craig?

21 Roy Thinnes (Alex Crown) once starred in a prime-time sci-fi series. What was it called?

22 Who is Danny Wolek's mother?

23 Who is the father of Victoria Buchanan's two sons?
A. Clint Buchanan
B. Joe Riley
C. Vince Wolek
D. Steve Burke

24 Before she joined the cast of *One Life to Live* as Joy O'Neill, Kristin Vigard played which very popular character on *The Guiding Light*?

25 To help clear Victoria of murder, Karen Wolek made a dramatic confession on the witness stand. What was it?

26 In what fictional Latin American country did several *One Life to Live* stories take place?
A. San Carlos
B. Santiago
C. San Raphael
D. San Pedro

Above: Samantha observes a confrontation between Will and Brad. Right: Maggie Ashley and Bo Buchanan.

PEYTON PLACE (1964-69)

1 Who was Allison Mackenzie's real father?
A. Elliott Carson
B. Martin Mackenzie
C. Leslie Harrington
D. Michael Rossi

2 How many marriages can Rodney Harrington and Betty Anderson total between them?

3 Who killed Elliott's first wife, Elizabeth Carson?
A. Leslie Harrington
B. Paul Hanley
C. Katherine Harrington
D. Elliott Carson

4 What happened to Ann Howard before she could marry Michael Rossi?

5 Rodney Harrington broke up with Betty after witnessing what event?

6 Which of these women was Leslie Harrington's sister?
A. Rita Jacks
B. Laura Brooks
C. Sandy Webber
D. none of the above

7 Which of these Peyton Place residents witnessed Elizabeth Carson's murder?
A. Constance Mackenzie
B. Leslie Harrington
C. George Anderson
D. none of the above

8 Which one of these famous actresses did not appear in *Peyton Place*?
A. Dorothy Malone
B. Barbara Rush
C. Lee Grant
D. Natalie Wood

9 Match the following characters with their occupations:
A. Michael Rossi
B. Paul Hanley
C. Eli Carson
D. Constance Mackenzie
E. Laura Brooks

1. manager of chandlery
2. nurse
3. manager of a bookstore
4. doctor
5. college teacher

10 Peyton Place launched the careers of the performers who played Allison Mackenzie and Rodney Harrington. Name them.

11 What was Matthew Swain's occupation?

12 Who was Steven Cord's real father?

13 Who was Norman Harrington initially in love with, and who did he finally marry?

14 Name the famous film star who played alcoholic Eddie Jacks.

15 Betty told Rodney that she was pregnant with his child in order to force him to marry her. True or False?

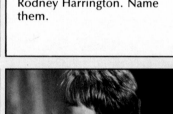

16 What two actors remained with *Peyton Place* from the first to last episode?

17 Julie Anderson had an affair with Leslie Harrington. True or False?

18 What caused Dr. Robert Morton to leave town?

19 What handicap was little Kim Schuster suffering from?

20 Who was Rodney accused of murdering?
A. Eddie Jacks
B. Paul Hanley
C. Stella Chernak
D. none of the above

21 What was Hannah Cord's occupation?

22 How, and why, was the character of Allison Mackenzie written out of the series?

23 The actress who played Claire Morton later made some very popular camera commercials. Name her, and her co-star on those commercials.

24 Katherine Harrington was murdered to prevent her from revealing a long-kept secret. True or False?

25 Name the firm run by Leslie Harrington and owned by his father-in-law.

Peyton Place residents Rita Jacks and Norman Harrington (top); Allison MacKenzie (left); Marsha Russell and Steven Cord (right).

RITUALS (1984-   )

1 Name the actress, best known for her role in the movie *M*A*S*H*, who originated the role of Taylor Chapin von Platen.

11 Prior to *Rituals*, Kin Shriner (Mike Gallagher) had become very popular with soap opera viewers through previous roles in two soaps. Name the soaps and the roles he played.

12 Who were Taylor's parents?

13 Name the girls' school where Lacey teaches.

14 In what town does *Rituals* take place?

15 Actor Monte Markham (Carter Robertson) guest starred in several *Dallas* episodes as Sue Ellen's lover. True or False?

2 What 1960s comedy series is the actress now playing Taylor best known for?

3 President Reagan's daughter, Patti Davis, had a brief role as Marissa Mallory. True or False?

4 What hit soap opera spoof of the mid-1970s starred Greg Mullavey, *Rituals'* Eddie Gallagher?

16 What ficticious South American country is Diandra Perez from?
A. Santiago
B. San Carlos
C. San Raphael
D. San Paulo

17 What is the name of the Chapins' family home?

18 Taylor von Platen was once married to Logan Williams. True or False?

5 Who is Greg Mullavey's famous real-life wife and what 1960s comedy hit did she star in?

6 What role did Andrea Moar (Julia Field on *Rituals*) play on *All My Children*?

7 George Lazenby, who plays Logan Williams, played which of these famous spies?
A. Napoleon Solo
B. Simon Templar
C. James Bond

19 Why was Lacey reluctant to marry Mike Gallagher?

20 What was the name of Julia's European lover who left her high and dry?

21 Katherine Chapin's will stipulated that Julia must meet a certain condition before she could receive her inheritance. What was it?

8 Brady Chapin and Taylor von Platen are brother and sister. True or False?

9 Mike Gallagher and Tom Gallagher are brothers. True or False?

10 Noelle Gallagher and Mike Gallagher are sister and brother. True or False?

22 On what daytime serial did Philece Sampler (Lacey) appear as Renee Dumonde?

23 Sara Gallagher once had an affair with Patrick Chapin. True or False?

24 Who was Eddie Gallagher's real father?

25 On what soap did Christine Jones and Peter Haskell (Christina and Carson Field in *Rituals*) co-star as husband and wife?

Top: Carter Robertson; Diandra Perez. Center: Jeff Robertson; Cherry Lane. Bottom: Lacey Jerrett-Gallagher; Mike Gallagher.

RYAN'S HOPE (1975-   )

1 Who played Lilly Darnell?

2 Who first played Bernard Levine?

3 Who pushed Frank down the stairs, and why?

4 How much money was Frank carrying when he was pushed down the stairs, and what was it for?

5 Who was blackmailing Frank?

6 Though Frank wanted to marry Jill, _____ forced him to change his mind and stay with Delia.

7 Who pushed Roger down the empty elevator shaft?

8 What happened to Roger after the fall?

9 On the show, how long did it take in air time for little Ryan to grow from a six-year-old to a teenager?

10 Pair the wives and husbands:
- A. Mary
- B. Maeve
- C. Siobhan
- D. Jill

1. Johnny
2. Frank
3. Jack
4. Joe

11 Where did Jacqueline find Sydney's revealing videotape?

12 Who was Prince?

13 Who was responsible for Prince's death?

14 Where did Maggie hide her diary from Max and Jacqueline?

15 Name the hospital where Roger and Seneca (among others) work.

16 How long was the sentence imposed on Seneca for pulling the plug on Nell's life support system?

17 Who is the father of Siobhan's baby?

18 Rae feared she had shot Michael, but who really killed him?

19 Why did Delia want Steve's paintings of her destroyed?

20 Name the TV station Leigh once owned.

21 After many months of searching for the broken gold coin, what did Max do with the four pieces?

22 Bess, Jill's mother, bakes _____ _____ to impress Matthew and others.

23 What name did Bess use when she returned to her daughter Jill?

24 To get even with Barry for kissing actress Lilly Darnell, Delia ran him over with her car. True or False?

25 To hide her affair with Roger, what excuse did Delia use to fool her husband Frank?

Maeve and Johnny Ryan (Helen Gallager and Bernard Barrow) head the Irish-American Ryan clan.

SANTA BARBARA (1984-   )

13 What did Peter install in the presidential suite of the Capwell Towers hotel?

14 C.C. Capwell earns most of his money from _____.

15 Why did C.C. hire Cruz?

16 Who is Brandon's mother?

17 Who is Brandon's father?

18 Who is raising Brandon as her son?

19 Who did Jade bump into at a Hollywood phone booth?

20 Before his long-awaited return to Santa Barbara, Lionel sent Augusta a giant _____.

21 Jade thought she was auditioning for a role in a Hollywood movie, but what was she really auditioning for?

1 Though the show is called *Santa Barbara*, it is actually set in Hollywood. True or False?

2 In what state is the sanatarium where Sophia Capwell was treated?

3 Who was first sentenced to prison for the murder of Channing Capwell, Jr.?

4 What natural disaster caused the death of Joe's father?

5 What did Peter place next to each of his murder victims?

6 What physical characteristic did Peter's victims have in common, and what was its significance?

7 What physical condition caused Peter to turn to murder for revenge?

8 After Joe was freed, who was next arrested for Channing's murder?

9 Who sang at the wedding of Joe and Kelly?

10 Ray Walston played a high-school teacher named Mr. Bumpers. True or False?

11 How did Ted manage to send his love notes to Laken?

12 Who made Amy pregnant?

22 Name the man Minx hired as her chauffeur.

23 What was that person's real job at the Lockridge house?

24 Who was hiding behind the beard and glasses of the mystery man, Dominick?

25 Name the first Capwell to realize that Sophia was still alive.

Above: Cruz Castillo and Eden Capwell (A Martinez and Marcy Walker). Right: Judith Anderson as Minx Lockridge.

SEARCH FOR TOMORROW (1951-   )

11 Who did Ellie run away with when she left her husband Stu?

12 Name Chase and Alec's TV teen dance show.

20 Who dragged T.R. to safety as a bomb exploded, killing Travis?

21 Who is T.R.'s real father?

13 Paralyzed by a bullet wound, Doug spent months in a wheelchair undergoing rehabilitation therapy, only to be disabled again in a car accident. True or False?

22 What piece of jewelry were singer Zach Anders and his manager Sylvie Descartes trying to steal?

23 Why did Jo divorce Martin Tourneur?

14 What happened to Jo when Sam returned to her life after being thought dead in Africa?

15 Who killed Sam after he kidnapped Jo?

24 Sunny turned to a well-known doctor to cure her brain tumor. True or False?

25 Who is the real father of Suzi's baby Jonah?

1 Who has played Jo Tourneur since the first day of broadcast?

5 Match the actress with the character she played:
A. Lee Grant
B. Morgan Fairchild
C. Susan Sarandon
D. Dody Goodman

16 Who pulled the plug on the paraplegic Doug?

17 Name Travis and Liza's company.

2 On a sunny day in August of 1983, *Search for Tomorrow* was broadcast live because the tapes of that day's show were missing. True or False?

1. Sarah Fairbanks
2. Althea Franklin
3. Rowe Peabody
4. Jennifer Pace Phillips

6 Name the motel Jo was running in the mid-1950s.

18 What is pilot Kentucky's last name?

19 What was Tante Helene's occupation?

3 Match the actor with the character he played:
A. Wayne Rogers
B. Vince O'Brien
C. Hal Linden
D. George Maharis

7 Who played Rose's mute brother Wilbur?

8 Why did Wilbur lose his voice?

1. Larry Carter
2. Bud Gardner
3. Slim Davis
4. Hal Conrad

4 What did the scheming Warren use to blackmail Brett?

9 Name the fictitious drug that Sam needed to control his blood disease.

10 How did Len save Grace Bolton's life?

Searching for tomorrow—top and lower right: Liza and Travis Sentell. Center: Jo Tourneur and second husband Arthur Tate.

THE SECRET STORM (1954-74)

1 What was Peter's relationship with Pauline Tyrell?

2 What initially prevented Amy from marrying Paul Britton?

3 What horrible shock did Susan Dunbar experience after she married Frank Carver?

4 Who was Susan later accused of murdering?

5 Match these characters with their occupations:
   A. Frank Carver
   B. Kevin Kincaid
   C. Ian Northcoate
   D. Hope Ames
   E. Jane Edwards

   1. painter
   2. lawyer
   3. newspaper person
   4. psychiatrist
   5. housekeeper

6 Who was the mother of Clay Stevens?
   A. Jill Stevens
   B. Lauri Hollister Reddin
   C. Robin Clemens
   D. none of the above

7 Which of these characters was revealed to be Dan Kincaid's illegitimate son?
   A. Kevin
   B. Robert
   C. Mark
   D. Alan

8 How did Jill and Hugh die?

9 How did Amy react when her husband left her?

10 Name Amy's three husbands.

11 What noted film actress filled in for her daughter for three days in the role of Joan Borman?
   A. Ingrid Bergman
   B. Joan Crawford
   C. Joan Bennett
   D. Bette Davis

12 Which of these teen idols of the early 1960s played R.B. Keefer?
   A. Frankie Avalon
   B. Tab Hunter
   C. Troy Donahue
   D. Fabian

13 Which of these famous actors played Bob Hill?
   A. Dustin Hoffman
   B. Jack Lemmon
   C. Roy Scheider
   D. Larry Hagman

14 What dual role was played by Gordon Ragsby?

15 How did Ellen Ames die?

16 What business was Pauline's family in?

17 What were the two local newspapers, and who ran them?

18 What "social problem" did Joanna Morrison finally overcome?

19 What actress, who later became popular as Carolee Aldrich on *The Doctors*, literally grew up on *The Secret Storm*?

20 Which one of these beautiful TV stars played Rocket?
   A. Donna Mills
   B. Morgan Fairchild
   C. Audrey Landers
   D. Pamela Sue Martin

21 The actor who played Erik Fulda later became an overnight daytime star as sexy Steve Frame on *Another World*. Who is he?

22 What actress, famous for her role in a classic children's fantasy film, played Katie?

23 With whom did Jerry Ames finally find happiness?

24 Who was the father of Amy's child Danielle?

25 Who was the father of Joanna's child?

Top: The cast of *The Secret Storm*. Center: Susan Ames Dunbar (Judy Lewis) and Frank Carver (Laurence Luckinbill).

TEXAS (1980-82)

1 *Texas* was a direct spin-off of the nighttime drama *Dallas*. True or False?

2 When Iris Carrington moved to Houston from Bay City, what happened to her personality?

3 How did Mike Marshall die?

4 Name the actor who played Mike Marshall.

5 Name the actor who played Mike's son Barrett.

6 Who took over as head writer during the last months of *Texas*?

7 Who shot Alex minutes after his wedding with Iris, and why?

8 Name the TV station Vicky Bellman owned.

9 Why didn't Vicky marry Hunt Weston?

10 Who left town so that Courtney could marry Jeb Hampton, and why?

11 Why did Courtney leave town?

12 Why did Jeb leave town?

13 When Iris again met Alex, the only man she had ever loved, how long had it been since their last meeting?

14 Who did Iris marry after Alex first vanished?

15 Who caused pregnant Ginny to miscarry?

16 Ginny and Ryan were divorced only months after their wedding. True or False?

17 After his marriage to Paige, what did Dennis learn about her?

18 After her marriage to Strikes, what did Vicky discover about her lawyer husband?

19 What did Reena bet Justin?

20 Who played the first leading lady of *Texas*?

21 Actor Damion Scheller played Gregory Linden Marshall. How old was he supposed to be?

22 Who played Mavis Cobb?

23 Eliot Carrington was a war correspondent covering the Vietnam War and earned a Pulitzer prize for his writing. True or False?

24 Who killed Alex, and why?

25 Who raped Dawn Marshall, and what became of her attacker?

Some of the characters whose stories are presented against a backdrop of "America's new heartland" in *Texas*.

WHERE THE HEART IS (1969-73)

1 *Where the Heart Is* took place in Northcross, Pennsylvania. True or False?

8 The nightclub owned by Ed Lucas was called the Starlight Lounge. True or False?

9 Who was Katrina Jessup's mother?

13 Peter Jardin witnessed a traumatic crime that he subsequently blocked out of his memory. What was it?

18 What was so controversial about the relationship between Christine Cameron and Tony Monroe?

19 What dreadful crime did Vicky Lucas commit?

2 Which of these daytime patriarchs portrayed Julian Hathaway?
   A. James Mitchell
   B. Bernie Barrow
   C. Jerry Douglas
   D. David Lewis

10 Which of these now famous actors once played a mugger on the show?
   A. Anthony Geary
   B. Christopher Reeve
   C. Larry Hagman
   D. William Devane

14 Steve Prescott suffered from:
   A. leukemia
   B. schizophrenia
   C. amnesia
   D. none of the above

20 Which of these Academy Award winning actresses portrayed Laura Blackburn?
   A. Ellen Burstyn
   B. Marsha Mason
   C. Jill Clayburgh
   D. Jessica Lange

3 What was Christine Cameron's occupation?

4 What was Julian's occupation?

5 Name Julian's two wives.

11 Stella O'Brien played the trumpet. True or False?

15 Kate Prescott suffered from:
   A. leukemia
   B. schizophrenia
   C. amnesia
   D. none of the above

21 How many actors portrayed Ed Lucas, and who were they?

22 Who was Daniel Hathaway?

6 What happened to Julian's first wife?

7 What two women were Julian and his son Michael involved with?

12 Which one of the following was John Rainey's ex-wife?
   A. Elizabeth Rainey
   B. Adrienne Harris
   C. Allison Jessup
   D. Mary Hathaway

16 What was the relationship between Kate and Roy Archer?

17 Julian Hathaway had two daughters: Kate and Allison. True or False?

23 With whom did Hugh Jessup have an affair while living with Christine?

24 How did Ellie die?

25 How did Roy Archer die?

Julian Hathaway, one of the central characters in *Where the Heart Is*—do you recognize the performer?

A WORLD APART (1970-71)

1 The character of Betty Kahlman was loosely patterned after veteran soap writer Agnes Nixon. True or False?

12 What role did David Birney play?

13 The family doctor's name was Jack Condon. True or False?

14 The director of this series was also a director of *The Guiding Light*. Name him.

15 Kathleen Maguire played conservative mother _____ _____.

16 Meg Johns was Betty Kahlman's:
  A. assistant writer
  B. older sister
  C. younger sister
  D. romantic rival

2 Which of these current stars did *not* play a role in this series?
  A. Susan Sullivan
  B. Clifton Davis
  C. Kevin Conway
  D. Donna Pescow

7 Who played easygoing, responsible Dr. Ed Sims?

8 Outside what major city was the story set?

11 Dorothy Lyman, *All My Children*'s wacky Opal Gardner, played another offbeat character, Julie Stark, on this series. Julie was a:

17 This show was sponsored by Procter & Gamble. True or False?

18 Russell Barry was the natural father of Patrice and Chris. True or False?

3 Name the confused teenager played by Susan Sarandon.

4 Who was the character played by former *All My Children* star Matthew Cowles?

9 Who were the three Sims children?

10 What role did former *All My Children* star Nicolas Surovy play?

  A. nymphomaniac businesswoman
  B. bag lady
  C. streetwalker
  D. hippie

19 One of the major themes that showed up in the storyline of *A World Apart* was that of the "generation gap." True or False?

5 Which pairing of role and performer is *incorrect*?
  A. Betty Kahlman— Augusta Dabney
  B. Betty Kahlman— Elizabeth Lawrence
  C. Russell Barry— Stephen Elliott
  D. Russell Barry— William Prince

6 Robert Gentry and Tom Ligon played roommates. True or False?

Two thoughtful threesomes from *A World Apart*. You should know the young actress pictured at top center.

1 What similar piece of information about their parentage did the characters of Ashley Abbott and Laurie Brooks Prentiss discover?

2 Michael Damian, who portrays rock singer Danny Romalotti, is a rock singer in real life. True or False?

3 What crime did Elizabeth Foster commit?

4 Name the autobiographical novel written by Laurie Brooks Prentiss that was based on her relationship with her sister Leslie.

5 Name the theme song of *The Young and the Restless*, which became famous in the 1976 Summer Olympics when a young Rumanian gymnast used the music to help her win a series of gold medals.

6 The son of a former U.S. president plays private detective Andy Richards. Name him.

7 Why does Kay hate Jill so much?

8 Learning that she was going to die, Vanessa Prentiss committed suicide but arranged for it to appear that Laurie had murdered her. True or False?

9 Which of these famous TV private eyes once played Jed Andrews?
  A. Jameson Parker
  B. Daniel Hugh-Kelly
  C. Lee Horsley
  D. Tom Selleck

10 What did Brooks sisters Chris and Peggy have in common?
  A. they were both in love with the same man
  B. they both wanted the same job
  C. they both discovered that another sister was adopted
  D. they had both been raped

11 What is Nikki's complete name?

12 What was the firm run by Ashley Abbott called, and how did it get that name?

13 Who prevented Ashley from marrying Eric Garrison?

14 Gina Roma is an ex-con. True or False?

15 Who was the one great love of Jack Abbott's life?

16 Jill was once married to Brock Reynolds, Kay's son. True or False?

17 What was contained in a sandwich that deadly Suzanne Lynch "innocently" served to Kay?
  A. poison
  B. a tarantula
  C. jewelry stolen by Kay
  D. a pebble

18 When Kay bought Derek Thurston his own beauty salon, it was on what conditions?

19 Match these characters with their health problems:
  A. Traci Abbott
  B. Nikki Reed
  C. Jennifer Brooks
  D. Leslie Brooks
  E. Kay Chancellor

  1. cancer
  2. alcoholism
  3. gonorrhea
  4. bulimia
  5. amnesia

20 Dina Abbott has two step-children, one of whom is Marc Mergeron. Who is the other?

21 Match these children to their fathers:
  A. Brooks Prentiss
  B. Charles Howard
  C. Heather Stevens
  D. Chuckie Rolland
  E. Laurie Brooks
  F. Ashley Abbott

  1. Paul Williams
  2. Snapper Foster
  3. Bruce Henderson
  4. Lance Prentiss
  5. Brent Davis
  6. Victor Newman

22 Why did Jack marry Patty?

23 Peggy had an affair with the unhappily married professor Jack Curtis. True or False?

24 What was Lucas's occupation before he came to Genoa City?

25 Danny married Traci because she was pregnant with his child. True or False?

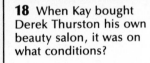
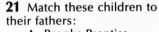

Left: Jack Abbott, Jill Foster Abbott, John Abbott. Above: Danny Romalotti. Top right: Lauren and Paul. **53**

'Til Death (or the Storyline) Do Them Part.

Getting married—and unmarried, and remarried—is one of the favorite pastimes of the characters who people the soaps. Here is a collection of wedding photographs from the world of soap opera. If you're a real soap fan, the first couple should be as familiar to you as your own family, but how many of the others do you recognize? The answers are on page 64.

ANSWERS

ALL MY CHILDREN
(Page 4)

1 Tad Martin, who saw Silver's photo in the local newspaper and recognized her as a girl he'd met on his travels.
2 Adam's insane twin brother, Stuart Chandler.
3 Adrian Shepherd
4 She is devoted to the cause of solar energy, and when Ellen and Mark bought their house it was heated by solar energy.
5 Zach used to be a gigolo, and the very wealthy Mrs. Colby was a client.
6 True; however, they *did* conceive a child after they were divorced.
7 *Raising Kane*
8 Connie Wilkes
9 The character was gay—a first for daytime television.
10 Toxoplasmosis
11 **A.** Sybil Thorne
12 Chuck and Donna's baby died in a fire.
13 Musical-comedy actor Robert Morse played Harry.
14 A football player.
15 The Cobra was Peg English, head of an international drug ring and Brooke's supposed mother. However, it was discovered later that Peg was not really Brooke's mother.
16 The Steampit
17 Lenny Wlasuk
18 She switched two wine glasses, one containing a lethal poison intended for her mother, so that her father (who had planted the poison) died instead.
19 Amy Tyler and Nick Brent.
20 He divorced her because he thought he was sterile, but he didn't tell her the reason.
21 David Thornton, Benny Sago, and Hank Ferguson.
22 **D.** None of the above. Andrew's real father was a stableboy employed by Chase Preston.
23 She called herself Monique Jonvil.
24 True
25 Christine Baranski, his real-life wife.

ANOTHER WORLD
(Page 6)

1 It was originally planned as a spin-off of her popular show, *As the World Turns*, hence *Another World*.
2 Agnes Nixon, creator of *All My Children* and *Loving*.
3 Actor Joe Morton, who actually sang on the daytime show.
4 Again, Joe Morton. Split-screen

techniques were used to show the actor in a dual role. (Abel was the one with the mustache.)
5 **A-4**, Alice Frame—doctor; **B-3**, Felicia Gallant—romance writer; **C-2**, Wallingford—mannequin repairperson; **D-1**, Perry Hutchins—cook.
6 Sculpting, as is actress Victoria Wyndham who plays the character.
7 Sandy and Blaine, Mac's son and daughter-in-law.
8 She discovered she was illegitimate. In Chicago, she was almost jailed for killing Danny Fargo.
9 Donna, who hides the fact that Marley is her illegitimate daughter by calling her her sister.
10 Cocaine; it drove him crazy and resulted in his committal to a mental institution.
11 Jealous of her father's love for Rachel, Iris tried to break up the couple by lying to her father that Rachel was unfaithful to him.
12 False; he was actually thrown clear, and he returned to Bay City many years later. He finally died in a car crash on his way to remarry Rachel.
13 He was Steven Frame, medically sound after recovering from the amnesia caused by the helicopter crash.
14 *A View from the Bay*, which was later produced as a movie in spite of its revealing nature.
15 A mesmerized nurse, Emily Benson, obeyed Carl Hutchins' orders and shot the doctor.
16 Larry's terminally ill mother, Jeanne Ewing. (The infant daughter of Larry and Clarice was named Jeanne after her paternal grandmother.)
17 Sixty; the move was a success and prompted networks to extend other soaps to the hour-long format. *Another World* was also the first soap to be expanded to 90 minutes.
18 *Brava* magazine, a publication owned by Mac Cory and Cory Publishing.
19 False; she wrote one novel while working for Felicia Gallant, but was brutally murdered by Ross, Carl's henchman, before she could score with another book.
20 She was a prostitute who took Ada's advice and quit walking the streets.
21 **A-2**, Perry—Smiley's; **B-3**, Lily—Tall Boys; **C-1**, Leo—The Warehouse.
22 Actor Brent Collins, who plays the character, is a dwarf.
23 Christopher Rich and Nancy Frangione, who play the once-married couple, are married in real life.

24 Publisher Cass Winthrop, who disguised himself as a woman to hide from Tony "the Tuna," a mobster to whom he owed money.
25 Sally, who had the child as the result of an affair. She eventually took custody of the boy after the Thatchers died.

AS THE WORLD TURNS
(Page 7)

1 False; she gave birth to quadruplets who were featured many times on the daytime drama.
2 They founded the Wade Bookshop. After Neil was hit by a car and died, Penny left town and Lisa managed the store.
3 He was going blind.
4 A slightly off-balance Dorothy Connors, the mother of Whit's illegitimate son Jay.
5 James Stenbeck is the father of Paul. Barb married him after fleeing the altar and Tom Hughes.
6 Her previous lover had died while they were making love.
7 **A-4**, Dr. Paul Stewart—Marco St. John; **B-1**, Dr. David Stewart—Henderson Forsythe; **C-3**, Dr. Doug Cassen—Nat Polen; **D-2**, Dr. Dan Stewart—John Reilly.
8 His experiences during the Vietnam War.
9 Elizabeth fell down the stairs, ruptured her liver, and died.
10 Paul Stewart, though most people believed Dan Stewart to be Betsy's father.
11 Noted TV star and celebrity Zsa Zsa Gabor.
12 To tend his stables.
13 **A-3**, Dr. Annie Ward Stewart—Mary Lynn Blanks; **B-2**, Dr. Susan Burke Stewart—Marie Masters; **C-1**, Nurse Pat Holland—Melinda Paterson; **D-4**, Nurse Lyla Montgomery—Ann Sward.
14 **A-2**, Martin Sheen—Jack Davis; **B-4**, Margaret Hamilton—Miss Peterson; **C-3**, Gloria DeHaven—Sara Fuller; **D-1**, James Earl Jones—Dr. Jerry Turner.
15 She left Oakdale to study law in California.
16 Gunnar Stenbeck, though Dustin thought Burke Donovan was his father.
17 He wanted to put James Stenbeck behind bars, but was foiled when Dee was accused of the supposed murder.
18 He faked a gunshot wound and then disappeared after Ellen found his supposedly bloody body.
19 Whit's valuable coin collection. Steve later proved his

innocence and Craig spent some time in jail.
20 The Green Fire necklace.
21 The storyline stated that Betsy had been disfigured in a car crash and had had plastic surgery, hence the "new" Betsy.
22 Tina Sloan; John Dixon knew this but concealed the truth so that he could be named chief of staff.
23 False; he committed suicide when he discovered that Natalie was having an affair with his own brother.
24 True; until then, all soaps were 15 minutes long.
25 Millionaire/publisher Lucinda Walsh is Sierra's real mother.

AS THE WORLD TURNS

BERRENGER'S
(Page 8)

1 A chic department store.
2 New York City
3 Tony Renaldi
4 Sarah
5 She accidentally killed her parents. While playing with matches as a child, she set her house on fire and her parents died in the blaze.
6 He was a shoe salesman.
7 Connie
8 David Berrenger was named after Paul's brother David.
9 He was killed in Vietnam.
10 True
11 John Higgins
12 **B.** Her ex-husband kidnapped their daughter Emily, and neither has been seen since.
13 He married Simon's granddaughter, Melody.
14 He was a clothing manufacturer.
15 A Treasury official on Danny Kruchek's payroll.
16 To hurt Simon Berrenger, who seemed interested in the lovely Laurel Hayes.
17 A sleazy factory owner, who forced himself on Babs Berrenger and Julio Morales as a silent partner in their designer clothing firm.
18 Vice president in charge of merchandising.
19 Ray Parker, composer of "Ghostbusters."
20 A video director.

21 False, although he admired her very much and wanted his son to stay married to her.

22 A conglomerate, owned by Danny Kruchek, which dealt in organized crime.

23 He blamed Simon for abandoning him and his mother, who was once Simon's mistress.

24 Because she was spying for a competitor.

25 Stacey

THE BEST OF EVERYTHING
(Page 9)

1 **C.** The serial was based on Rona Jaffe's novel of the same name.

2 Patty McCormack, who as a child made an indelible impression on movie audiences as an evil little girl in the 1956 film *The Bad Seed*.

3 The series recounted the stories of several career girls.

4 **B.** Gale Sondergaard played Amanda Key. Agnes Moorehead never appeared on a soap; Joan Fontaine was on *Ryan's Hope* for a short time; and Joan Crawford once filled in for her daughter Christina on *The Secret Storm* when Christina was ill.

5 Geraldine Fitzgerald

6 New York City

7 False; Julie Mannix's daughter is Danielle von Zerneck, who played Louisa Swenson on *General Hospital*.

8 True

9 He was reported killed in Africa.

10 At Metropolitan Hospital.

11 True

12 False; she was left barren and for a time, almost crippled.

13 He was a high-school English teacher.

14 **A.** Key Publishing; in the original novel the company was called Fabian Publications.

15 He was editor of a news magazine called *Today*.

16 Because he was constantly unfaithful to her.

17 Kate Farrow

18 Medford Center

19 He was an advertising executive.

20 Dexter Key

21 A young boy almost died when he ate tainted candy; Kim was accused of manufacturing LSD and putting it into the candy.

22 *SHE* magazine, which was similar to such publications as *Glamour* and *Mademoiselle*.

23 **A.** Barnard

24 When Kim almost died, Eddie realized the strength of his feelings for her.

25 A tape in the possession of Dexter's mother, Amanda, which revealed a horrible secret about Kim. Eddie had been seeing April before he fell in love with Kim, and was forced to state, untruthfully, that he was the father of April's baby in order to prevent Amanda from revealing the tape's contents and destroying Kim. Viewers never learned what was actually on the tape because the serial went off the air before the episode revealing the secret was aired. According to the script, however, the tape was to reveal that Kim's natural father had been a criminal.

CAPITOL
(Page 10)

1 True; she is married to John Gavin, ambassador to Mexico.

2 Carolyn Jones played the role until her death in 1982.

3 Myrna vowed revenge when Clarissa married Myrna's true love, Baxter McCandless, some 30 years ago.

4 She caused Clarissa's father, Judson, to be framed as a Communist sympathizer and tossed out of Washington.

5 The highly rated *The Young and the Restless*.

6 False; Tyler is an Air Force vet with the record of a hero.

7 Lawrence Barrington; Myrna wanted to keep the Cleggs and the McCandlesses apart.

8 Julie had amnesia at the time and believed every word her mother said.

9 He was a penniless man who posed as wealthy Lawrence Barrington in order to insinuate himself into the Clegg family— and fortune.

10 Gymnastics; this occurred before the 1984 Olympics, but the writers eventually dropped the storyline.

11 Gambling, especially cards.

12 He lost Julie, his true love, to his older brother.

13 Jordy wanted his sister Julie to marry Tyler, whom she really loved, rather than Lawrence.

14 In his parent's cabana, which he had redecorated and turned into a high-class bachelor pad.

15 True; the payoff was also intended to keep Trey from knowing about his son's relationship with Shelley.

16 Kelly changed her name—she was the Shelley who had taken Myrna's $100,000 on the understanding that she would leave town.

17 Scotty

18 N'shoba, where he and Sloane were held prisoner for a while.

19 **D.** *Capitol Focus*

20 Chip, the former manager of Corky's bar.

21 The factory worker and union leader dated Jordy Clegg, who was using the name Jay to hide his true identity.

22 True; many viewers think that actor Michael Catlin is really paralyzed, but he's not.

23 Kelly Harper, but it was an accident.

24 Myrna witnessed the shooting. To save her reputation, she was later forced to arrange for the case to be closed.

25 True; she claimed to be suffering from agoraphobia, but a brain tumor was later revealed to have caused her mental instability.

DALLAS
(Page 12)

1 **B.** Southworth (Wentworth is the last name of Pam's sister, Katherine.)

2 **D.** Holly Harwood

3 Three: Francine Tacker, Morgan Fairchild, and Priscilla Presley.

4 Kristin Shepard

5 Katherine Wentworth

6 False; the late Jeff Faraday, one of Kristin's many lovers, was Christopher's father.

7 **A.** Roger, who raped her when she refused his advances.

8 That Dusty was really the illegitimate son of Clayton's deranged sister Lady Jessica.

9 The Southern Cross

10 True

11 Hutch McKinney, the Ewings' former foreman.

12 Dave Culver is Donna's stepson from her first marriage to Sam Culver. Kristin Shepard was Sue Ellen's vindictive younger sister. Katherine is Pamela's vindictive younger sister. Mickey Trotter was Ray Krebbs' cousin.

13 False; it was revealed that J.R. was John Ross's real father.

14 Renaldo Marchetta

15 **A-3**, Larry Hagman—*I Dream of Jeannie*; **B-4**, Susan Howard—*Petrocelli*; **C-2**, Patrick Duffy—*Man From Atlantis*; **D-1**, Jennilee Harrison—*Three's Company*.

16 **C.** Ava Gardner, who appeared on *Knots Landing*. Martha Scott portrayed Sue Ellen's mother; Barbara Bel Geddes was the original Miss Ellie; and Alexis Smith played Lady Jessica.

17 Mickey's mother, although Ray stood trial for the murder.

18 True

19 Mandy claims she picked Cliff up on the night Bobby Ewing was shot, but Cliff's first memory of the beautiful model was when she appeared at the courthouse to clear him of the attempted murder charge.

20 False; Renaldo Marchetta is Charlie's father.

21 The Store

22 Steve

23 Miss Young Dallas

24 Because she discovered he was going to die.

25 True

DARK SHADOWS
(Page 14)

1 If Adam died, Barnabas would revert to being a vampire.

2 **C.** "Quentin's Theme"

3 **A-2**, Quentin—werewolf; **B-3**, Cassandra—witch; **C-1**, Tom—vampire; **D-4**, Beth—ghost.

4 A race of blob-like creatures that lurked in the village of Collinsport.

5 Klaus von Bulow, convicted of trying to murder his wife, socialite Sunny von Bulow.

6 Dr. Lang was the only man who, through his experiment with Adam, was able to "cure" Barnabas of being a vampire.

7 To wipe out witchcraft.

8 **B.** Alexandra Moltke only played governess Victoria Winters; the rest of the cast portrayed various parts.

9 True; somehow, Peter's love for Victoria transcended time and he wound up in the 20th Century as Jeff Clark.

10 False; he was Roger's son and Cassandra's stepson.

11 Through a dream curse started by Angelique.

12 Warlock Nicholas Blair, because he desired Maggie for himself.

13 Her love for Barnabas Collins.

14 He worked for Barnabas. He did all Barnabas's dirty work on the threat of being sent back to the institution where he'd been interred.

15 Beth Chavez

16 The charismatic Mr. Selby is now wreaking havoc on *Falcon Crest*.

17 Victoria Winters

18 False; it appeared as if she had been burned, but at that moment she was transported back into the 20th Century from which she'd come.

19 Angelique

20 Nicholas Blair turned Angelique from a witch into a female vampire because her obsession with Barnabas Collins interfered with his schemes.

21 Barnabas murdered the maniacal Reverend by walling him up alive.

22 The Blue Whale

23 When they found themselves in the year 1995 they discovered that Collingsport had fallen into ruins, so they went back in time to prevent that from happening.

24 A parallel time, containing people who looked exactly like the residents of Collinsport but had different names.

25 They were played by Jonathan

ANSWERS

Frid and Lara Parker, whom viewers identified with as enemies Barnabas Collins and Angelique. Seeing the actors now play lovers was a bit unsettling for the audience, and that aspect of the storyline helped lead to the show's demise.

DAYS OF OUR LIVES
(Page 16)

1 Shenanigans
2 Chris and Danny.
3 **A-4**, Tom Horton—Alice; **B-2**, Doug Williams—Julie; **C-1**, Roman Brady—Marlena; **D-3**, Mickey Horton—Maggie.
4 He wanted to use her money to pay off his gambling debts.
5 Blondie's
6 University Hospital
7 Leukemia
8 False; Roman stopped her romantic advances before she could take him to bed.
9 A raven's feather.
10 Andre Di Mera; Jack Kositchek was the Salem Strangler.
11 True
12 True
13 Marlena treated Fred for his wife-beating problem.
14 Angel
15 Bill Hayes, who also played Doug.
16 An hourglass.
17 MacDonald Carey, playing Tom Horton.
18 False; rock lyricists Tommy Boyce and Bobby Hart write many of the songs.
19 **D.** All three actors have played the role.
20 Kate Winograd and Linda Anderson.
21 Madame X
22 True; and before she became a nun, Marie was a drug addict.
23 The death of their son D.J.
24 He fell off a cliff during a struggle with the evil Stefano.
25 He drives a motorcycle.
26 Stefano had faked his own death and "returned," so he chose as his symbol the phoenix, a mythical bird which was believed to have risen from its own ashes.

THE DOCTORS
(Page 17)

1 Hope Memorial Hospital
2 He was a brain surgeon.
3 Ten
4 Kathleen Turner, star of *Body Heat* and *Romancing the Stone*.
5 False; she played Dr. Kate Bartok. At the time she was known as Ellen McRae, not Ellen Burstyn.
6 True; the nurses were on the set to make sure the operating

equipment was laid out correctly.
7 It was the only soap opera that did not begin as a serial.
8 *The Doctors* was the first soap to win an Emmy award.
9 **A-3**, Sam Shafer—hospital chaplain; **B-4**, Pete Banas—hospital custodian; **C-2**, Brock Hayden—cattle baron; **D-1**, Toni Ferra—lab technician.
10 She divorced her husband and the chaplain, Sam, hid his own feelings for her.
11 His gangster brother used illegally obtained money to finance Nick's education.
12 False; Liz took the drug and the "trip" almost made her jump off a ledge.
13 Buddy died of spinal meningitis.
14 He was shot by one of his psychopathic patients.
15 Ann caught Obonda fever.
16 Dr. Tom Barrett, Nick's medical school friend.
17 True; she played a model by the name of Elizabeth Harrington. Shields and other celebrities such as James Coco made brief guest appearances in an attempt to bolster the ratings, but the show was cancelled anyway.
18 The middle-aged couple demanded $5,000.
19 The psychotic Kathy Ryker kidnapped Stephanie.
20 The show was dedicated to the brotherhood of healing.
21 A blood clot was causing Althea to go blind.
22 True—thanks to a mysterious elixir of youth which enabled Adrienne's 60-year-old mother, Felicia, to pose as her own daughter. Both Adrienne and Felicia were portrayed by actress Nancy Stafford.
23 Dr. Paul Summers
24 An elderly schoolteacher found the tape.
25 San Francisco; but Althea found her and brought her home, and Nick's operation saved her life.
26 He was a pediatrician.
27 Glenn Corbett

DYNASTY
(Page 18)

1 **B.** *Oil*
2 She was a secretary at his firm.
3 Matthew Blaisdel
4 **B.** Daniel Reece is Sammy Jo's father. Cecil Colby is Jeff's late uncle; Mark Jennings is Krystle's late first husband; Hank Grant is a well-known reporter for *The Hollywood Reporter*.
5 He was living in Billings, Montana, unaware of his real identity until his "grandmother" revealed that

she kidnapped him as an infant.
6 Blake was accused of murdering his son's lover, Ted Dinard.
7 He is the only bisexual character on prime time (or for that matter, daytime) television.
8 Matthew Blaisdel; he and their daughter were killed in Africa.
9 To prevent her father from going bankrupt, she agreed to marry Cecil Colby's nephew. In return, Cecil would bail her father out.
10 She was supposedly killed in a plane crash with Peter DiVilbus. (However, she should turn up alive shortly, if she hasn't already!)
11 Alexis, pregnant when she and Blake separated, kept Amanda's existence a secret because she was afraid that Blake would take the child away, as he had their other children.
12 Fallon and Jeff Colby.
13 Sammy Jo and Steven Carrington.
14 True
15 Of a heart attack (while making love with his new bride, Alexis).
16 False; Nicole only pretended they were married.
17 Five: Steven, Fallon, Adam, Amanda, and Kristina.
18 Adam
19 La Mirage
20 **A-3**, James Farentino—Nick Toscanni; **B-1**, John Saxon—Ahmed Rashid; **C-2**, Helmut Berger—Peter DeVilbus; **D-4**, Paul Burke—Neil McVane.
21 **C.** Neil McVane
22 She died in a mental institution.
23 True
24 Plagued by recurring headaches, the result of an earlier accident, Fallon disappeared from her own wedding and was later presumed dead.
25 **D.** Lady Ashley Mitchell

THE EDGE OF NIGHT
(Page 20)

1 False; they were the same person—Serena suffered from a split personality.
2 Perry Mason
3 In a car accident while trying to save her little girl, Laurie Ann.
4 She mistook him for her husband, Kirk.
5 Duane Stewart, Adam Drake, and Miles Cavanaugh.
6 True; she was about the only virgin over the age of 20 to be found in soaps.
7 False
8 She was being drugged by Benedict, one of the attendants.

9 Raven was having an affair with her future stepfather, Ansel Scott.
10 She was mistaken for Nicole Drake, the intended victim.
11 Clay Jordan, Nicole's doctor.
12 Margo Dorn
13 While trying to kill Liz Hillyer, Elly Jo fell out of the speeding car and was killed instantly.
14 Held captive on Limbo Island.
15 Because Chris Egan—and the audience—believed that Alicia was dead.
16 Mark Aldrich kidnapped Raven because he mistook her for his dead wife.
17 She accidentally caused the death of one of her patients, Maria Hathaway, by striking her so that she fell and hit her head.
18 The very respectable Geraldine Whitney killed Logan. (She mistook him for a burglar, and only found out the truth months later.)
19 They were committed by Emily Michaels' maid, Molly Sherwood. She poisoned tea meant for Draper's wife April, but Nadine drank it instead. Then, when Eliot Dorn suspected the truth, she killed him, too.
20 Because her father, the notorious Anthony Saxon, was on the other side of the law—he ran a crime syndicate.
21 They learned that they were not really brother and sister, which meant there was nothing to stop them from getting married.
22 She had been a hooker.
23 Morlock, who worked for the crime syndicate. All those people had to be eliminated because they were a threat to the syndicate.
24 McGrath's
25 Upon learning that young Timmy Faraday had been kidnapped, Nancy, fearing for the boy's safety, went through her husband's files and leaked information to handsome Beau Richardson. Mike thought she was having an affair with Richardson, and Nancy couldn't tell him the truth.

FALCON CREST
(Page 22)

1 They are half brothers; they have the same mother, Jacqueline Perrault, but different fathers.
2 They all have the same father, Douglas Channing.
3 They are cousins; Chase's father was the brother of Angela Channing, Emma and Julia's mother.
4 *The Globe*
5 **C.** Angela arranged the

marriage so she could get her hands on the Agretti harvest.

6 The late Douglas Channing, Richard's father and Angela's first husband.

7 That Maggie was adopted.

8 That Melissa had become barren as the result of an accident.

9 **A-2**, Linda Caproni—Cole Gioberti; **B-3**, Angela Channing—Philip Erikson; **C-4**, Victoria Gioberti—Nick Hogan; **D-1**, Stephanie Hoffman—Richard Channing.

10 Julia Cumson

11 Julia Cumson

12 Gustav Reibmann arranged both.

13 Wine production.

14 Gina Lollobrigida

15 **B.** Barbara Bel Geddes—she used to be Miss Ellie on *Dallas*.

16 Johann Reibmann and Jacqueline Perrault.

17 Joel McCarthy

18 Linda Gioberti, Philip Erikson, and Dr. Michael Ranson, all of whom were newly married. (In fact, getting married on *Falcon Crest* may be the kiss of death!)

19 *The Vintage Years*

20 True

21 Jason Gioberti

22 Francesca sold him her share of the winery.

23 False; she's his stepdaughter.

24 **A.** Shannon Tweed

25 **A-5**, Nick Hogan had an affair with his ex-wife after marrying Victoria Gioberti for her money; **B-4**, Gustav Reibmann was a murderer who also arranged his father's death; **C-3**, Charlotte Pershing was a gambler; **D-2**, Terry Ranson was a call girl; **E-1**, Joel McCarthy was a drug addict.

FLAME IN THE WIND/A TIME FOR US
(Page 24)

1 Driscoll

2 **D.** Kate Austen; she wrote the sort of novel real-life novelist Grace Metalious had given the reading public with *Peyton Place*.

3 *Flame in the Wind*; when the show became *A Time For Us*, that story was dropped and the romance between Steve and Jane became prominent.

4 Havilland

5 Reynolds

6 Chris Austen

7 True; they all played Linda Driscoll.

8 **B.** Rita Lloyd played Leslie Farrell; Maggie Hayes played Roxanne Reynolds.

9 Joseph Hardy

10 Craig was Roxanne's ex-husband.

11 Dave Simon

12 Anne Revere

13 False; Leslie was Roxanne's stepmother.

14 Miriam Bentley

15 **B.** Roy Poole

16 False; she was the story editor.

17 Doug Colton

FLAMINGO ROAD
(Page 25)

1 **A.** Truro, Florida

2 Lute-Mae, the town madame.

3 Titus

4 She was a singer with a slightly shady past; she had once worked in a carnival.

5 *The Clarion*, run by Elmo Tyson.

6 True, although Constance thought Claude and Eudora had adopted her. While he was married to Eudora, Claude had a brief fling with Lute-Mae and Constance was the result. Claude and Eudora adopted the baby, but it was years before Eudora learned that Claude was, in fact, Constance's natural father.

7 False; the unhappily married Eudora had a brief affair with Elmo, resulting in Skipper, but she passed off the child as Claude's.

8 He was in the construction business.

9 **B.** Field Carlyle, who only married her because her family's money could help him further his political ambitions.

10 She fell over a stair railing during an argument with Field.

11 He was the town sheriff and resident bad guy.

12 He was a victim of Titus's scheme to sabotage *The Clarion*, which had printed an anti-gambling article written by Skipper.

13 **D.** All of the above.

14 They were brother and sister.

15 Julio's sister Alicia, a beautiful Cuban.

16 Michael Edwards

17 **A.** and **D.** Sandy, terrified of her brother's ruthlessness, was about to confess all to Field. In an attempt to stop her, Michael employed a voodoo practice and burned a picture of her. Shortly afterwards she had a car accident, and while she was in the hospital Michael asked Julia to make sure Sandy didn't talk. Julia instructed a servant to turn off Sandy's life support system and Sandy died.

18 Titus, the sheriff.

19 False; the marriage was postponed several times but they did finally marry, and Lane was expecting Sam's child

when the show ended.

20 **D.** Sam Curtis

21 Flamingo Road was the most extravagant street in town and living there was a symbol of success.

22 He was a politician.

23 True; his first wife was Vanessa Curtis.

24 Sandy worked for *Tallahassee Today* magazine.

25 Joan Crawford

FROM THESE ROOTS
(Page 26)

1 *The Strathfield Record*

2 Laura Tompkins

3 **B.** Ben, Jr. became a farmer.

4 Emily's son Tim married Nate's daughter Peggy.

5 False; Liz's niece, Lyddy Benson, was involved with the wheelchair-bound Don Curtiss.

6 True; viewers were shown backstage scenes including dressing rooms and the director's control room.

7 Bruce Crawford

8 Playwright David Allen

9 **D.** Dr. Buck Weaver was played by Tom Shirley.

10 Maggie Barber

11 In the New England town of Strathfield.

12 Richard, one of two young brothers Buck and Maggie adopted.

13 Emily was married twice—to Jim Benson and Frank Teton.

14 **A.** Fred Barnes was a banker.

15 Stanley Kreiser

16 False; she played adoption agent Hilda Furman.

17 She was an alcoholic.

18 Craig Huebing

19 **D.** Joseph Mascolo, who plays Stefano Di Mera on *Days of Our Lives*. Larry Bryggman plays Dr. John Dixon on *As the World Turns*; David Canary plays Adam Chandler on *All My Children*; James Mitchell plays Palmer Cortlandt on *All My Children*.

20 The Poplars

21 Actress Lynn Franklin

22 **A.** Tom Jennings was a theatrical director.

23 Rose Corelli

24 They ran a farm.

25 True

GENERAL HOSPITAL
(Page 27)

1 Andrei Chernin

2 True; she is descended from an Aztec princess.

3 So that Ginny wouldn't launch a custody suit for his adopted son Mike, and so that the boy would live with his real mother.

4 **A-3**, Jeff Webber—Steve Hardy; **B-1**, Laura Spencer—Gordon Gray; **C-2**, Martha Taylor—Phil Brewer; **D-4**, Jimmy Lee Holt—Edward Quartermaine.

5 True; she accidentally killed David Hamilton and let her mother Lesley take the rap for it.

6 Sally (in drag) was really hit man Max who was hired to kill Luke and Laura.

7 "Uncle Miltie" himself, Milton Berle.

8 False; her mother, Alice Grant, killed Diana.

9 Steven Lars Webber; needing money, Steven's mother sold her son to the black market, and lied to her husband that the child was dead. The boy was later adopted by the Taylors.

10 Laura was held prisoner by Stavros Cassadine.

11 To give a name to her child by Luke, who was presumed dead, and to avoid being deported to England.

12 It was a synthetic diamond from which the formula for making synthetic diamonds could be extracted. That same formula could also be used to manufacture carbonic snow, by which the world's temperature—and, thus, the world—could be controlled.

13 June Lockhart, star of *Lassie* and *Lost in Space*.

14 True

15 Their religious affiliations. She was an Irish Catholic, he was an Orthodox Jew.

16 True; his parents' marriage is invalid because Lila never got a legal divorce from her first husband.

17 The late Susan Moore was Jason's mother.

18 Prostitution; Bobbie was a prostitute and Ruby was a madame.

19 They come from the same country.

20 Because she thought his brother Rick, the real love of her life, was dead.

21 **C.** Jackie Templeton

22 Alcohol

23 The DVX

24 **A-5**, Slick Jones—cab driver; **B-4**, Delfina—dressmaker, **C-3**, O'Reilly—spy; **D-1**, Emma Lutz—dizzy housewife; **E-2**, Stella Fields—housekeeper.

25 True; but it was an accident.

THE GUIDING LIGHT
(Page 28)

1 True; when actress Charita Bauer learned that she was going to be a mother on the show she requested that the

ANSWERS

child be named Michael after her own newborn son.

2 **A.** Janet Mason, who had a torrid affair with Ed but never married him.

3 Janet's husband, Ken Norris, mistakenly believed that Janet had resumed the affair with Ed which had been broken off before she married Ken, and he shot Ed in a fit of blind anger.

4 **B.** Josh; Reva had an affair with Josh and when that romance broke up she married Billy, whom she later divorced. She resumed her affair with Josh, but it didn't work out that time, either, and eventually Reva married H.B., father of both Josh and Billy.

5 Justin and Jackie Marler. A complicated plot twist had Jackie Marler give birth to a son and Elizabeth Spaulding give birth to a stillborn child at the same European hospital. Jackie didn't want her baby, and Alan Spaulding desperately wanted a male heir, so Alan arranged to pass off Jackie's baby as his and Elizabeth's. Alan didn't know who the baby's real parents were, and it was years before Elizabeth learned that Phillip was not her natural son.

6 Kelly Nelson

7 Selby Flats and Five Points.

8 Leslie Jackson, Ed's first wife.

9 A mysterious person was paying Susan to get rid of the Reardons. The reason? A murder had been committed in the cottage long ago and the body was still buried in the cellar.

10 **B.** Elizabeth Spaulding; the couple were deeply in love but never married because Phillip couldn't accept Mike as his father.

11 Brandon Luvonecjek

12 False; she is Alexandra's niece.

13 Sean Ryan

14 **A-4**, Amanda Spaulding—Alan Spaulding; **B-2**, Christina Bauer—Roger Thorpe; **C-1**, Victoria Tamerlaine—Brandon Spaulding; **D-5**, Billy Fletcher—Marty Dillman; **E-3**, Stacey Reardon—Floyd Parker.

15 **D.** Christopher Reeve, who appeared on *Love of Life*. In *The Guiding Light*, Billy Dee Williams and James Earl Jones both played Dr. Jim Frazier; Christopher Walken played Michael Bauer as a child (he was then known as Glenn Walken).

16 **A.** Jobeth Williams starred as Brandy Shelloe. The other three actresses appeared on *Search for Tomorrow*.

17 Martha

18 False; she's divorced from Andy Norris.

19 Her mother worked as the housekeeper for the Lewis family back in Tulsa, where both the Shayne and the Lewis clans lived before moving to Springfield.

20 India's father, Baron von Halkein, was once married to Alexandra.

21 He raped his stepdaughter, Beth Raines.

22 Leslie Ann's husband Warren caused her death. Slimy Warren was so intent on discovering the cure for the "dreaming death" disease which was plaguing Springfield that he broke into Jim Reardon's laboratory and accidentally set free some mice that were infected with the disease. One crept into his suitcase and crawled out in Warren's home, where it later bit Lesley Ann. She died before Jim Reardon had discovered the cure for the disease.

23 Jim posed as Dr. Jim Stephens in order to keep his research secret. He locked himself up in his lab day and night and refused to meet anyone who might remember him as one of Bea Reardon's children. He also kept his presence in town secret from his family, until the truth finally came out.

24 Leslie Norris, Stanley's wife, stood trial for his murder, but the actual killer was Marion Conway, the mother of Stanley's secretary.

25 False; Beth and Phillip were never lovers.

HOW TO SURVIVE A MARRIAGE
(Page 29)

1 **C.** Julie was a psychiatrist.

2 Rosemary Prinz

3 **C.** Tony DeAngelo

4 **A.** Ken Kercheval, who plays Cliff Barnes. Larry Hagman, now the one and only J.R. Ewing, was on *Edge of Night* for years; the other two *Dallas* actors were never on daytime soaps.

5 The characters were both Jewish, an almost unheard of phenomenon on soaps at the time.

6 He was a clothing manufacturer.

7 **C.** His business was going under or, to put it more succinctly, he was going broke.

8 Larry was having an affair.

9 **B.** Rachel

10 **A.** Armand Assante

11 Maria McGhee

12 Joan Copeland, a renowned stage actress in her own right.

13 It was the first "relevant" show to talk openly about sex, divorce, and problems that many women faced but did not discuss.

14 Steve Elmore and Berkeley Harris. Berkeley Harris, who died recently, was married to Beverlee McKinsey, a well-known daytime actress who currently stars on *The Guiding Light*.

15 **B.** Brad Davis, who became an "overnight" star with the feature film *Midnight Express* and who recently starred on television as Robert Kennedy. Daniel Travanti had a brief role on *General Hospital*; Tom Selleck played Jed Andrews on *The Young and the Restless*; and William Devane appeared as a mugger on *Where the Heart Is*.

16 He died of a heart attack, leaving his wife and daughter almost penniless.

17 **D.** Albert Ottenhiemer played Moe. Albert Hague currently stars on the TV series *Fame*; Lou Jacobi appeared on *Somerset* for a while; and Albert Stratton starred as Tom Donnelly on *Love Is a Many Splendored Thing*.

18 **D.** Elissa Leeds

19 False; Julie was single.

20 A while after *How to Survive a Marriage* ended, Jennifer Harmon turned up as Cathy Craig on *One Life to Live*.

21 He portrayed Scooter Warren, Laura Avery's boss and would-be lover on *Knots Landing*.

22 Fans of *The Doctors* will remember Lauren White as nurse M.J. Match.

23 Three: Michael Landrum, Ken Kercheval, and Michael Hawkins.

24 He was the original Frank Ryan on *Ryan's Hope*.

25 False; Fran never remarried after her husband's death.

KNOTS LANDING
(Page 30)

1 Alcohol

2 Daniel, named after his newborn son.

3 She was hired by Abby Ewing to distract Gary. (Abby noticed her amazing resemblance to the late Ciji Dunne.)

4 Abby's late brother, Sid Fairgate, was Karen's first husband.

5 **D.** Joshua Rush; at the time of writing, anyway.

6 True

7 *Capricorn Crude*

8 A wily criminal who came to town and was trying to become a publicist. He romanced rich

Diana Fairgate while having an affair with Ciji Dunne, then accidentally killed Ciji and was later killed himself.

9 Both roles are played by Lisa Hartman.

10 Howard Duff

11 Greg Sumner

12 Through Greg Sumner's "connections."

13 Julie Harris

14 Mack was the D.A. investigating the death of Karen's husband.

15 He was killed in a car crash arranged by the "organization."

16 **A-4**, Diana's mother is Karen Mackenzie; **B-1**, Joshua's mother is Lilimae Clements; **C-2**, Olivia's mother is Abby Ewing; **D-3**, Greg's mother is Ruth Galveston.

17 A crime syndicate run by Mark St. Clair.

18 She took a murder rap for her husband Ray.

KNOTS LANDING

19 Unable to believe that her twins were dead, Val developed amnesia, blocked out the trauma, and took the name of one of the characters in her second novel. Val felt "at home" living in Shula under the guise of Verna.

20 **C.** Knots Landing Motors

21 He was killed by the Wolfbridge Group—although their intended victim was Gary.

22 He works as a journalist for Abby Ewing's cable station.

23 Gary has been married three times, twice to Val, once to Abby.

24 Michele Lee (Karen), Ted Shackelford (Gary), Constance McCashin (Laura), and Joan Van Ark (Val).

25 She tried to kill Chip Roberts when she learned he had lied to her.

LOVE IS A MANY SPLENDORED THING
(Page 32)

1 Leslie Charleson played Iris and now plays Dr. Monica Quartermaine on *General Hospital*.

2 The novel came first.

3 The movie, released in 1955.
4 True, but this plot was canceled by the head of programming.
5 True; Mia was an Eurasian woman in love with an American doctor.
6 The head of CBS programming ordered the love affair cut out of the soap to avoid the risk of offending viewers.
7 Noted TV sitcom and programming head, Fred Silverman.
8 He thought she was his wife, Laura.
9 He performed an illegal abortion, and she found out about it.
10 **C.** She left town.
11 **D.** All of them.
12 He was a successful architect.
13 **B.** Donna Mills
14 Julie killed him by accident and left town because of it.
15 Her real name was Martha, and she changed it after becoming an actress.
16 As a result of brain injuries sustained in a plane crash.
17 Yes; Dr. Peter Chernak operated on her using a revolutionary laser beam treatment.
18 A tape naming the real father of Spence and Iris's baby, little Maggie.
19 In spite of the tape, Spence won. Iris confessed the name of the father, thus rendering the blackmail attempt ineffective.
20 Millionaire Walter Travis
21 **B.** David Birney
22 Laura and Mark adopted a child.
23 Dr. Jim Abbott, who had returned to town and was in love with Iris.
24 Laura Donnelly
25 **D.** San Francisco

LOVE OF LIFE
(Page 33)
1 **D.** Kevin Kline; however, he did appear on *Search for Tomorrow.*
2 **B.** Marsha Mason; the other three actresses appeared on daytime dramas, but only Mason starred in *Love of Life.*
3 Barbara Sterling Latimer
4 Because he needed his mother's approval in order to inherit a large amount of land, and she promised to give it to him after he married Betsy.
5 Ben Harper was jailed for bigamy. Before marrying Betsy, he had already wed Arlene Lovett, but had kept their marriage a secret so he could get the land his mother had promised him.
6 He played Humphrey Bogart. Jerry Lacy, who played Rick Latimer, bore such an uncanny

resemblance to Bogart that he was given many roles in which he imitated the actor.
7 **B.** Dan Phillips, Kate's husband. For a time, however, it appeared that Rebecca's father was Rick Latimer, who had raped Kate one night. When Kate became pregnant as a result, nurse Candy Lowe, who was in love with Dan, faked a blood test so that Rick would appear to be the baby's father.
8 Barrowsville
9 Rosehill
10 **C.** Gaye Sterling
11 **B.** John Dennis
12 Paul Raven and Bruce Sterling.
13 True; in one of the most graphic daytime scenes ever, Ben Harper was gang-raped by his fellow prison inmates.
14 Christopher Reeve
15 Ben Harper and Cal Aleata.
16 It was discovered that he was none other than Vanessa Sterling's first husband, Paul Raven, whom she believed was dead.
17 **C.** Charles Lamont
18 **C.** Sally Bridgeman—although Jamie had been involved with all of them.
19 He was accidentally shot by his wife Felicia, who mistook him for an intruder.
20 He killed his father, Jeff Hart, after Jeff had tried to rape David's girlfriend, Cal Aleata.
21 **B.** Kate Swanson; **D.** Meg Hart. Neither Kate nor Meg married Rick.
22 **B.** Ian Russell; Arlene later married Ray Slater, who renounced his unscrupulous ways and brought April up as his own daughter.
23 True; Felicia died while giving birth to Eddie's child.
24 Bruce Sterling
25 He raped her when she refused to sleep with him.

LOVING
(Page 34)
1 True, though the two-hour special used him only to attract evening audiences to the daytime show that would follow.
2 Swimming
3 Dane Hammond, who was anxious to use her and her father's identity to outbid Alden Enterprises on construction projects.
4 Cabot Alden, who is also the father of Ann Alden Forbes Hammond.
5 He was dean of the University.
6 Lily; she was accused of shooting her father in her bedroom.
7 June, angry at her husband for raping their daughter and causing her to turn to alcohol

LOVING

for solace shot him.
8 WCN; she later moved to another station in Washington, D.C.
9 She was a volunteer during his election campaign.
10 His airplane crashed over Africa, but his body was not found.
11 He jumped off the Golden Gate Bridge. His body wasn't found, either.
12 **A-2**, Noreen—nurse; **B-3**, Billy—coach; **C-4**, Rose—seamstress; **D-1**, Soames—butler.
13 She stole his keys.
14 An eye mask to keep the light out.
15 Penny, the waitress at the Hideaway.
16 Dooley's
17 Drama and communications. He eventually moved out west to write TV shows.
18 While in Washington with Ann, Mike visited the Peace Memorial.
19 Dane Hammond, but he didn't know it until Jack told him.
20 Father Jim Vochek, who almost left the priesthood because of her.
21 She became pregnant and wouldn't have an abortion.
22 After they were married, she did have an abortion.
23 It was their term for making love.
24 Billy appeared to be sterile.
25 Three, though Stacey is somewhat embarrassed by the fact.

MARY HARTMAN, MARY HARTMAN
(Page 36)
1 It was a spoof or satire of soap operas.
2 Fernwood, Ohio
3 He was "flashing," or briefly opening his coat to reveal that he was wearing nothing underneath. Larkin was known around town as The Fernwood Flasher.
4 **B.** Mary Kay Place played

Loretta. Glenn Close never appeared in soaps; Jobeth Williams starred in *Somerset* and *The Guiding Light*; Sigourney Weaver (the only one of the four who did not also appear in *The Big Chill*) never had a recurring soap role.
5 He collapsed of a heart attack and was taken to the hospital, where he and Mary finally made love.
6 **C.** Loretta Haggers, Mary's best friend.
7 Vivian Blaine, who became famous for her role as Adelaide in *Guys and Dolls.*
8 False; they were gay, and they pretended to be brothers so they could live together without anyone taking much notice.
9 He saw a documentary on Mary, in which Mary's daughter, Heather, remarked that her mother was having affairs with two men and had thrown her drunken father out of the house.
10 With his young son, he headed a religious organization known as the Worldwide Missionary Crusade.
11 He accidentally shot himself in the groin instead of shooting Merle Jeeter, who had trapped Loretta in his hotel room.
12 *Fernwood 2-Night*
13 **D.** Cathy Shumway
14 Dabney Coleman, who also played Jane Fonda's boyfriend in the movie *On Golden Pond.*
15 He desired Cathy Shumway and ran off with her.
16 **A.** Typical American Consumer Housewife.
17 He accidentally locked himself in a closet and was stabbed to death by a Christmas decoration which plunged into his back.
18 He was kidnapped and brainwashed by the Hare Krishnas, but later returned home.
19 True
20 She had "adopted" Pat Gimble, who, having been cleared of murder, returned home. To fill the gap, devastated Zorina then kidnapped Cathy's baby from a laundromat.
21 That Wanda, Merle, and their maid Lila had had a ménage à trois!
22 Louise Lasser
23 By threatening to reveal to the Reverend's wife her husband's liaison with Florence Baedeker.
24 The murder of the Lombardi family.
25 Who knows? Cathy certainly didn't!
26 She wanted to be a country singer.
27 In a bowling alley lounge.

ANSWERS

28 She was in a car accident.
29 She wound up in a hospital mental ward.
30 It was explained that George had fallen into a vat of chemicals at the factory where he worked. After plastic surgery he was (literally) a new man.

ONE LIFE TO LIVE
(Page 38)
1 Three
2 Joe Riley, Steve Burke, and Clint Buchanan.
3 **B.** Asa Buchanan is Bo's real father. For a while, however, both Asa and Bo believed that Yancy Ralston, with whom Olympia Buchanan once had an affair, was Bo's real father.
4 False; Larry has been married three times—to Meredith Lord, and to two women named Karen.
5 She was a novice nun. However, Jenny eventually renounced her vows and got married. To date, in fact, she's been married four times!
6 Dr. Joyce Brothers
7 *Laredo*
8 Actor Jameson Parker is currently starring in the CBS hit, *Simon and Simon.*
9 The baby was conceived by Samantha and Rafe Garretson, but shortly before Samantha died the embryo was transplanted into Delilah's womb.
10 Sammy Davis, Jr.
11 **B.** David Renaldi is Cassie's real father. Victor Lord was the father of Meredith, Victoria, and Tony Lord, and was recently revealed to be Tina Clayton's father as well. Clint Buchanan has no children of his own. Herb Callison, who was married to Cassie's mother at the time Cassie came back into her life, adopted Cassie.
12 Nikki Smith was Victoria Lord's alter ego. Torn between her domineering father and macho Joe Riley, Victoria developed a split personality. Nikki was common, coarse and free-spirited—quite different from Victoria herself.
13 Both actresses returned to the roles they created after other actresses had taken over their parts.
14 Lazlo Braedeker was played by Walter Slezak, real-life father of *One Life to Live* actress Erika Slezak (Viki). He had a one-day role as Viki's godfather.
15 Wanda used to be married to Larry's brother, who died.
16 **D.** Bo Buchanan is Drew's father. Asa is Drew's adoptive

father and Bo's real father; Drew Ralston was once engaged to Drew's mother; and Clint is Bo's brother.
17 Arlene Dahl
18 True; Marco and Mario were brothers. For a time Gerry portrayed Marco impersonating Mario, who was murdered. During that time, it was believed that Marco, not Mario, had been killed.
19 Tommy Lee Jones; he won an Emmy for *The Executioner's Song.*
20 Carla, a light-skinned black who passed for white, was the daughter of the hospital cleaning lady, Sadie Gray—although Jim had no idea that they were related.
21 *The Invaders*
22 Meredith Lord Wolek
23 **B.** Joe Riley
24 Kristin Vigard played Morgan Richards on *The Guiding Light.*
25 Karen, happily married to prominent doctor Larry Wolek, (Viki's brother-in-law) confessed that she was a prostitute, and that while out with a "john" she had discovered that he was the real murderer. Karen had purposely withheld this information until the last minute, knowing that it would destroy her marriage.
26 **A.** San Carlos

PEYTON PLACE
(Page 40)
1 **A.** Elliot Carson
2 Six; twice to each other, and once each to other people.
3 **C.** Katherine Harrington; although Elliot Carson was convicted of the crime and spent 18 years in jail for it.
4 She fell over a cliff and was killed.
5 He saw his father in the arms of his secretary, who happened to be Betty's mother, and assumed they were having an affair.
6 Laura Brooks
7 **D.** None of the above. Twelve-year-old Paul Hanley witnessed the crime, or so he thought.
8 **D.** Natalie Wood, although her younger sister, Lana, did appear on the show.
9 **A-4**, Michael Rossi—doctor; **B-5**, Paul Hanley—college teacher; **C-1**, Eli Carson—manager of a chandlery; **D-3**, Constance Mackenzie—manager of a bookstore; **E-2**, Laura Brooks—nurse.
10 Mia Farrow and Ryan O'Neal.
11 He was publisher of Peyton Place's newspaper.
12 Martin Peyton
13 He first fell in love with Allison, but later found happiness with Rita Jacks.

RYAN'S HOPE

14 Dan Duryea
15 True
16 Ed Nelson who played Michael Rossi, and Christopher Connelly who played Norman Harrington.
17 False
18 He realized that he had made a wrong diagnosis which eventually cost one of his patients his life.
19 She was deaf.
20 **D.** None of them. He was accused of killing Stella's brother, Joe.
21 She was housekeeper to Martin Peyton.
22 Allison supposedly ran off to New York, never to be heard of again. In real life, Mia Farrow left the show to marry Frank Sinatra.
23 Mariette Hartley; her partner on the Polaroid commercials was James Garner.
24 False; she died a natural death.
25 Peyton Mills

RITUALS
(Page 41)
1 JoAnn Pflug
2 Tina Louise, who currently plays Taylor, is known for playing Ginger Grant on *Gilligan's Island.*
3 True
4 *Mary Hartman, Mary Hartman;* he played Mary's husband Tom.
5 Meredith MacRae, who starred as Billie Jo Bradley in *Petticoat Junction.*
6 Carrie Sanders
7 **C.** George Lazenby played James Bond in *On Her Majesty's Secret Service,* the only 007 movie in which the secret agent married.
8 True
9 False; Mike is Tom's uncle.
10 False; Mike is Noelle's uncle.
11 Kin Shriner played Scotty Baldwin on *General Hospital,* then portrayed Jeb Richmond on *Texas.*
12 Katherine and Patrick Chapin.
13 Haddon Hall
14 Wingfield
15 True
16 **A.** Santiago
17 The Willows
18 False; they were lovers but did not marry.

19 Because she found out he'd slept with Diandra.
20 Bernhardt Kraus
21 That she remain in Wingfield for at least one year.
22 *Days of Our Lives*
23 True
24 Patrick Chapin
25 They co-starred as husband and wife Hollis and Catsy Kirkland on *Ryan's Hope.*

RYAN'S HOPE
(Page 42)
1 Christine Ebersole, who later starred on NBC's *Saturday Night Live.*
2 Bruce Weitz, *Hill Street Blues'* Mick Belker.
3 His wife Delia when he asked for a divorce so that he could marry Jill.
4 $6,500; the money was intended to pay off a blackmailer.
5 Roger, who had found out that Frank, who was married to Delia, was having an affair with Jill.
6 Jill, who didn't want to cause the end of Frank's political career.
7 Frank, although Maggie may have also had a hand in it because the three were struggling at the time of the accident.
8 He injured his hand and could no longer operate.
9 About six months. The producers wanted to bring another young character onto the show and quickly "aged" the girl.
10 **A-3**, Mary—Jack; **B-1**, Maeve—Johnny; **C-4**, Siobahn—Joe; **D-2**, Jill—Frank.
11 In the basement, inside the videotape machine.
12 Prince was Max's butler.
13 Hutch; Prince discovered his scheme to ruin Max and died because of it.
14 In a hiding place above the canopied bed.
15 Riverside Hospital
16 One week. Letters were found revealing that Nell wanted to die.
17 Joe Novak, who was married to Jacqueline.
18 Mobster Sal Brooks, who shot the man *after* Rae had shot him initially.
19 They were nude studies that he used to blackmail her and her husband Matthew.
20 WTJ
21 As Jill watched, shocked, he tossed them into the ocean.
22 She bakes sticky buns.
23 Betsy; she assumed another name to find out what Maggie was doing with Jill.
24 True; he survived the accident and promised not to press

charges if she would stop drinking.

25 She claimed she was going to a Chinese cooking school with a new friend called Sheila.

SANTA BARBARA
(Page 44)

1 False; it's set in Santa Barbara and uses many actual on-location scenes to showcase the town.
2 Alaska; however, everyone thought the woman was dead.
3 Joe Perkins; he didn't commit the crime, but he served five years for it before being released.
4 An earthquake.
5 A white carnation—which is why he was called the Carnation Killer.
6 They all had blonde hair. He imagined all of them to be Kelly, the blonde woman he was once engaged to.
7 An aneurysm. He refused to take any medicine to control its debilitating effects.
8 Lionel was arrested for the crime, although he insisted that he was innocent.
9 Singer Jeffrey Osborne, who sang a couple of his popular hits.
10 True
11 He used homing pigeons—until Laken's mother killed one and served it for dinner.
12 Jeff; he wanted her to have an abortion to free him of his responsibility, but she refused.
13 A one-way mirror, to be used for spying on guests. It was built into a utility closet.
14 Oil, he has wells all over the California coast.
15 To douse an out-of-control fire on an oil rig.
16 Santana Andrade, though she vowed never to reveal the relationship to the little boy.
17 The late Channing Capwell is Brandon's father.
18 Gina DeMott, whose own child died at birth.
19 David Hasselhoff, star of the TV show Knight Rider.
20 Lionel sent Augusta a sarcophagus. He's an expert in archeology.
21 A porno film. The innocent teen was saved by her boyfriend Danny.
22 Brick Wallace
23 Minx really hired Brick to handle the family stock portfolio.
24 Sophia Capwell, who assumed the disguise in order to frame Lionel for Channing's murder.
25 Eden; suspecting that the wig and glasses were a disguise, Eden pulled them off and

revealed "Dominick" to be her mother.

SEARCH FOR TOMORROW
(Page 46)

1 Former B-movie starlet Mary Stuart plays Jo.
2 True; it was the first time in more than five years that a soap had been performed live.
3 A-3, Wayne Rogers—Slim Davis; B-4, Vince O'Brien—Hal Conrad; C-1, Hal Linden—Larry Carter; D-2, George Maharis—Bud Gardner.
4 A pornographic videotape which starred Brett.
5 A-3, Lee Grant—Rose Peabody; B-4, Morgan Fairchild—Jennifer Pace Phillips; C-1, Susan Sarandon—Sarah Fairbanks; D-2, Dody Goodman—Althea Franklin.
6 The Motor Haven; she used the money to support her little girl.
7 Actor/comedian Don Knots played Wilbur.
8 He became mute as a reaction to almost killing his foster father, who had tried to molest his sister Rose.
9 Hemadol; Andrea tried to sneak him an overdose in a drink, but almost died herself when the drinks were switched.

SEARCH FOR TOMORROW

10 He used a bent spoon to remove a fish bone on which she was choking.
11 She ran off with the Inn's chef and hasn't been heard from since.
12 Knights of the Turntable
13 True; when drunk, Len hit the car and caused the newly rejuvenated Doug to be paralyzed from the neck down.
14 Her blindness returned. This time it was psychosomatic because she was in love with Tony.
15 George and Sarah found the couple in the mountain cabin and shot and killed Sam.
16 Jennifer and Hal, though Jennifer did it for Scott's sake, while Hal did it to keep his embezzling from being discovered.
17 Tourneur Instruments

18 Bluebird
19 She was a psychic who tried to help Nick kill Liza.
20 Lloyd Kendall, the mysterious newspaper publisher.
21 Lloyd Kendall
22 An expensive jade necklace that Travis had given Liza.
23 After they were married she discovered that he was addicted to gambling and alcohol.
24 False; her doctor, Winston Kyle, was actually a quack who almost caused her death by prescribing herbs and health foods for a cure.
25 Warren Carter is the real father. Suzi, however, wants Cagney to help her raise her child.

THE SECRET STORM
(Page 47)

1 He had once been engaged to Pauline, but he married her sister Ellen instead.
2 He was already married.
3 She learned that her first husband, Alan, was alive.
4 Alan Dunbar, who was actually killed by drug dealers.
5 A-3, Frank Carver—newspaperman; B-2, Kevin Kincaid—lawyer; C-4, Ian Northcoate—psychiatrist; D-1, Hope Ames—painter; E-5, Jane Edwards—housekeeper.
6 A. Jill Stevens
7 B. Robert
8 In a plane crash.
9 She became so distraught that she almost suffered a nervous breakdown.
10 Kip Rysdale, Paul Britton, and Kevin Kincaid.
11 B. Joan Crawford (Joan Bennett starred in Dark Shadows but the other two actresses never appeared on soaps.)
12 C. Troy Donahue
13 C. Roy Scheider; Larry Hagman played Ed Gibson on The Edge of Night for years, but the other two never appeared on soaps.
14 Dr. Ian Northcoate and his insane twin brother, Owen.
15 She died in a car accident.
16 They owned Tyrell's, the local department store.
17 The Clarion, run by Arthur Rysdale, and The Herald, run by Peter Ames.
18 Joanna overcame drug addiction.
19 Jada Rowland, who played young Amy Ames.
20 A. Donna Mills, who is now on Knots Landing. Morgan Fairchild was on Search for Tomorrow; Audrey Landers played Joanna Morrison on The Secret Storm, then Heather Kane on Somerset; Pamela Sue

Martin never appeared on a daytime soap but did appear on Dynasty.
21 George Reinholt
22 Margaret Hamilton, who played the Wicked Witch of the West in The Wizard of Oz.
23 With Hope Crandall Ames, his second wife.
24 Her doctor, Brian Neeves.
25 Her boyfriend, Robert Landers.

TEXAS
(Page 48)

1 False; it was a spin-off of Another World.
2 The conniving woman suddenly became a warm and understanding lady—but viewers didn't like the new Iris.
3 He committed suicide after his oil company failed.
4 Stephen D. Newman
5 The same actor, Stephen D. Newman.
6 Actress Pamela Long Hammer, who played Ashley Linden Marshall on the show.
7 Eliot, who hated the fact that Alex was his real father.
8 KVIC-TV
9 He admitted that he was a priest, and she convinced him to stay in the priesthood.
10 Kevin; Courtney couldn't decide between Jeb and Kevin, so Kevin decided for her.
11 After Kevin left town, her romance with Jeb fell apart.
12 To find Courtney, the love of his life.
13 Twenty-five years.
14 Eliot Carrington, who thought that he was the father of their son Dennis.
15 Barrett, her husband, who discovered that her pregnancy was the result of an affair and went into a rage.
16 False; Ryan was killed in a plane crash.
17 Dennis learned that his new wife had starred in many porno films before he knew her.
18 Vicky discovered that he was a bigamist with another family south of the border.
19 She bet him that she would put Marshall Oil out of business in six months; if she didn't, she would sleep with him. She lost the bet.
20 Beverlee McKinsey
21 Ten years old.
22 Dody Goodman, star of other daytime dramas and of The Jack Paar Show.
23 False; he was a correspondent who was believed to have been killed in action but who later returned to wreak havoc in the lives of Iris and Alex.
24 The mob found out that he knew about their illegal activities within his oil company and had him killed.

ANSWERS

25 Ex-con Billy Joe Wright. He eventually cleaned up his life and tried to go straight and, in fact, became a TV star.

WHERE THE HEART IS
(Page 50)

1 False; it took place in Northcross, Connecticut.
2 **A.** James Mitchell, who now portrays the inimitable Palmer Cortlandt on *All My Children*. Bernie Barrow plays Johnny Ryan on *Ryan's Hope*; Jerry Douglas portrays John Abbott on *The Young and the Restless*; and David Lewis is Edward Quartermaine on *General Hospital*.
3 She was a photographer.
4 He was an English professor.
5 Elaine and Mary Hathaway.
6 She committed suicide.
7 Julian's second wife, the much younger Mary Hathaway; and Elizabeth Rainey, who while living with Michael became pregnant with his father's child.
8 True
9 Christine Cameron
10 **D.** William Devane, who now plays Senator Gregory Sumner on *Knots Landing*. Anthony Geary played a mentally disturbed individual on *Bright Promise* and a rapist on *The Young and the Restless* before becoming an overnight sensation as antihero Luke Spencer on *General Hospital*; before becoming Superman, Christopher Reeve portrayed Ben Harper on *Love of Life*; Larry Hagman, *Dallas*'s J.R. Ewing, portrayed Ed Gibson on *The Edge of Night*.
11 False; the Hathaway clan's eccentric housekeeper played the bugle, not the trumpet.
12 **B.** Adrienne Harris was John Rainey's ex-wife. Elizabeth Rainey was his daughter; Allison Jessup was Hugh Jessup's wife; and Mary Hathaway was Julian's second wife.
13 His aunt Margaret killed her brother, for whom she had incestuous feelings, when he refused to leave his wife; Peter Jardin saw the murder.
14 **C.** Steve Prescott developed amnesia after being left for dead by criminals.
15 **B.** Kate developed schizophrenia after her adopted son, Peter Jardin, was killed.
16 Roy was married to Kate's sister Allison, but had been romantically involved with Kate years earlier.
17 False; Kate and Allison were Julian's sisters.

18 Tony, a married man, was living with Christine. Back in the early 1970s, it was quite a novelty for a soap opera to present such a relationship.
19 She pushed Mary Hathaway down a flight of stairs!
20 **B.** Marsha Mason portrayed Laura Blackburn. Ellen Burstyn starred as Dr. Kate Bartok on *The Doctors*; Jill Clayburgh played Grace Bolton on *Search for Tomorrow*; and Jessica Lange was never on a soap.
21 Three; Mark Gordon, Charles Cioffi, and Joseph Mascolo.
22 Judge Daniel Hathaway was Julian's father and Michael's grandfather. He died right before the show began, and his death set the story in motion.
23 His own wife—Allison Hathaway Jessup.
24 Ellie Jardin was killed by criminals for giving shelter to Steve Prescott.
25 Roy Archer was killed by a mugger, played by William Devane.

A WORLD APART
(Page 51)

1 False; Katherine L. Phillips created Betty in the mold of her mother, queen of the soap writers Irna Phillips.
2 **D.** Donna Pescow
3 Patrice Kahlman
4 Chris Kahlman
5 **C.** Russell Barry was played by William Prince; Stephen Elliott was played by Jack Condon.
6 True
7 James Noble
8 Chicago
9 Bill, Becky, and Sarah.
10 Fred Turner
11 **D.** Julie was a hippie.
12 Oliver Harrell
13 False; the family doctor was Nathaniel Fuller.
14 The late Walter Gorman.
15 Adrian Sims
16 **A.** She was her assistant writer.
17 False; ABC owned the show.
18 False; Betty Kahlman adopted the two children before she married Barry.
19 True

THE YOUNG AND THE RESTLESS

THE YOUNG AND THE RESTLESS
(Page 52)

1 They both learned that their adored fathers weren't really their fathers.
2 True
3 At his request, she "pulled the plug" on her dying husband Bill; she couldn't bear to see him in such pain.
4 *In My Sister's Shadow*
5 "Nadia's Theme"
6 Steven Ford, Gerald Ford's son.
7 Years ago, Jill stole Kay's husband, Phillip Chancellor, and Kay has never forgiven her.
8 True
9 **D.** Tom Selleck, better known as *Magnum, P.I.* Jameson Parker, now of *Simon and Simon*, appeared on *Somerset* and *One Life to Live*; Daniel Hugh-Kelly of *Hardcastle and McCormick* starred on *Ryan's Hope*; and Lee Horsley, star of *Matt Houston*, never appeared on a soap.
10 **D.** They had both been raped.
11 Nikki Reed Foster Bancroft DiSalvo Newman...so far.
12 Jabot Cosmetics, derived from the name of its owner, Ashley's father John Abbott.
13 The very French and debonair Marc Mergeron stole Ashley's heart, so she couldn't go through with her wedding to Eric.
14 True
15 Model Diane Jenkins Richards, who left town upon realizing that she didn't love her husband and that the man she did love, Jack, was a cad.
16 True
17 **B.** A tarantula was in the sandwich.
18 That he forget about Jill Foster and stay married to Kay for one year. In return Kay would see to it that Jill's illegitimate son would be provided for.
19 **A-4**, Traci Abbott—bulemia; **B-3**, Nikki Reed—gonorrhea; **C-1**, Jennifer Brooks—breast cancer; **D-5**, Leslie Brooks—amnesia; **E-2**, Kay Chancellor—alcoholism.
20 Marc's sister, Danielle Mergeron.
21 **A-4**, Brooks Prentiss—Lance Prentiss; **B-6**, Charles Howard—Victor Newman; **C-1**, Heather Stevens—Paul Williams; **D-2**, Chuckie Rolland—Snapper Foster; **E-3**, Laurie Brooks—Bruce Henderson; **F-5**, Ashley Abbott—Brent Davis.
22 To secure the presidency of Jabot Cosmetics, which his father promised him if he wed Patty.

23 False; she was in love with him, but they never consummated their love until they were married.
24 He was a sailor.
25 False; he married her to give her illegitimate child a name, but he wasn't the father. She later lost the baby.

'TIL DEATH (OR THE STORYLINE) DO THEM PART...
(Page 54)

1 *General Hospital*'s Laura and Luke Spencer (Genie Francis and Anthony Geary).
2 Betsy and Steve Andropolous (Meg Ryan and Frank Runyeon) on *As The World Turns*.
3 The remarriage of Daisy and Palmer Cortlandt (Gillian Spencer and James Mitchell) on *All My Children*.

DYNASTY

4 The remarriage of Nola and Jason Aldrich (Kim Zimmer and Glen Corbett) on *The Doctors*.
5 Julie and Doug Williams (Susan Seaforth Hayes and Bill Hayes) remarry on *Days of Our Lives*.
6 *All My Children*'s Jenny Gardner and Greg Nelson (Kim Delaney and Laurence Lau).
7 Cathy Geary and Joshua Rush (Lisa Hartman and Alec Baldwin) on *Knots Landing*.
8 Myra Murdock and Jasper Sloane (Elizabeth Lawrence and Ronald Drake) on *All My Children*.
9 Morgan and Kelly Nelson (Jennifer Cook and John Wesley Shipp) on *The Guiding Light*.
10 Lane Ballou and Sam Curtis (Cristina Raines and John Beck) on *Flamingo Road*.
11 Jenny and David Reynolds (Brynn Thayer and Michael Zaslow) on *One Life to Live*.
12 Blaine Ewing and Sandy Cory (Laura Malone and Chris Rich) on *Another World*, married in a joint ceremony with:
13 *Another World*'s Rachel Davis and Mac Cory (Victoria Wyndham and Douglass Watson), who were remarrying.
14 Sue Ellen and J.R. Ewing (Linda Gray and Larry Hagman) from *Dallas*—of course.